GW00750738

Guide to Inner Light

Guide to Inner Light

by
Taoist Master
Ni, Hua-Ching

The Shrine of the Eternal Breath of Tao
College of Tao and Traditional Chinese Healing
LOS ANGELES

My appreciation to George Robinson, Frank Gibson and his Atlanta Center and Janet DeCourtney for proofreading, typing and editing this book.

Hua-Ching Ni

Shrine of the Eternal Breath of Tao, Malibu, California
College of Tao and Traditional Chinese Healing
117 Stonehaven Way
Los Angeles, CA 90049

Copyright 1990 by Ni, Hua-Ching.
Library of Congress Catalog Card Number 90-060825
ISBN 0-937064-30-0
All rights reserved.

This book is dedicated to those who shall receive
the Inner Light from learning the experience of millions
of years of spiritual development and the achievements
of some special sages in the integral spiritual truth.

To female readers:

According to Taoist teaching, male and female are equally important in the natural sphere. This is seen in the diagram of Tai Chi. Thus, discrimination is not practiced in our tradition. All my work is dedicated to both genders of human beings.

Wherever possible, use of masculine pronouns to represent both sexes is avoided. Where it occurs, we ask your tolerance and spiritual understanding. We hope that you will take the essence of my teaching and overlook the triviality of language. Gender discrimination is inherent in English; ancient Chinese pronouns do not have the difference of gender. I wish all of you might achieve yourselves above the level of language or gender.

Thank you, H. C. Ni

CONTENTS

PREFACE

Developing the wholeness of human nature is a natural goal. What do the words "wholeness of nature" mean? They describe the unison of an individual's spirit, mind, body, intellect and heart, and that of the entire human society. Together, they work in one direction: to make practical progress which comes back to serve our lives.

However, in the recent 2,000 years of human development, those parts all seemed to go separate ways. In the Middle Ages, people experienced religious dominance. Later, the Renaissance brought back the awakening of artistic and literary humanistic expression. However, scientific exploration still remained suppressed until these two most recent centuries. So the division of the mind, heart and spirit became wider; each went its own way. It is a painful and troubled experience to have such contradiction where the human mind cannot enjoy its whole development.

But isn't there another way of human experience? Is there an experience, a teaching for humans which does not suffer an internal split between past and future? Can we, living in this modern time based on the dominance of materialism, also find a way to fulfill our spiritual development?

With true spiritual development, your mind and intellect will not conflict with your heart and spirit any more. Your physical expansion in its correct function is also recognized by your own spirit. This is what I present: the experience of the Taoist Integral Way. In this book, we can work together to review human growth and find the important unity within and without. We shall see no conflict between different religions, cultures and lifestyles. We live with our hearts and at the same time we live with our minds.

Besides this book, my recent work under other titles, *Essence of Universal Spirituality* and *Internal Spiritual Growth Through Learning Tao* will help you rise above the fragments of different experiences, joining them together to support our new life, new generation, new time, new hope and new future. I am sure you will enjoy reading and using them, thus eliminating the need for excessive personal work and research. Through this way, you can reach and enjoy where you should be.

Your spiritual friend,
Ni, Hua-Ching

PRELUDE

"Tao is the destination of all religions, while it leaves behind all religions just like the clothing of different seasons and different places. Tao is the goal of serious science, but it leaves behind all sciences as a partial and temporal description of the Integral Truth.

"The teaching of Tao includes all religious subjects, yet it is not on the same level of religions. Its breadth and depth go far beyond the limits of religion. The teaching of Tao serves people's lives like religions do, yet it transcends all religions and contains the essence of all religions.

"The teaching of Tao is not like any one of the sciences. It is above the level of any single subject of science.

"The teaching of Tao is the master teaching of all. However, it does not mean the teaching relies on a master. It means the teaching of Tao is like a master key which can unlock all doors leading to the Integral Truth. It teaches the truth directly or shows the truth directly. It does not stay on the emotional surface of life or remain at the level of thought or belief. Neither does it stay on the intellectual level of life, maintaining skepticism and searching endlessly. The teaching of Tao presents the core of the subtle truth and helps you to reach it yourself."

INTRODUCTION:
BEING ONESELF

Visitor: Master Ni, your teaching is helping. I have been struggling in general. It has become a habit since the bad life experience of my early years. This struggling harms my spiritual growth; please enlighten me further.

Master Ni: The most sensitive part of life is the spirit. It is the center of a person's life. When a person's spirit has no connection with general struggle in life, no real gain is made. I mean, when the spirit has no connection with struggle, struggling brings no real gain to a person's life; it results in loss.

All lives have the possibility of maintaining their connection with spiritual life. Many people lose themselves in the flow of life or movement of worldly matters. Instead of moving upward and forward, they sink downward and backward, and they lose their connection with their own spiritual life. All life comes from the great life. All life enjoys the oneness of the great life.

The majority of people lose their spiritual vision by establishing a false mind. Keeping a false mind maintains separation from truth; it causes struggle. A person who does that loses himself. A person who attains spiritual awakening regains his spiritual life, eternal life. A person who attains the great awakening of life always keeps his mind as the central foundation of his being; he keeps his mind in clearness, quietude, joy and unity. He does not dare separate his mind from its rightful unity with his inner spirit. People who do this practice of maintaining unity pray to maintain clarity, quietude, truth, beauty and goodness.

The above attainment which I have described is a whole connection; it is a description of the whole thing. I hope that

I have done the job of giving this simple but meaningful instruction of the guidance of the achieved ones.

Q: Could you please tell me, what is the source of life?

Master Ni: The life of the universe is one life. On the material level, each individual is like the land: each piece can be separated by the ocean. But the subtle essence of life and the universe penetrates everything. That is the true life.

Let us talk about it in this way. What connects with your physical body? Physical life has birth and death. It is not wise to suffer during your life. If you suffer in your life, it is because you create a false knowledge of contention and you struggle for small things. You do not see the eternal essence of life which is always there. If you learn the eternal essence, you will realize that the small gain is not worth your struggle or contention.

For example, you might think you have a problem with your sister, parents or someone else; but actually, there is no problem. It is all either your stubbornness or their stubbornness. If they are being stubborn, they think, "You are my daughter so you must be such and such a way, as I desire. If you are my sister, you must be the sister that I desire. If you are my worker, you have to be the kind of person I desire." If you are being stubborn, you think the same thing, only vice-versa. So the other person has his stubbornness from his false mind or false conception, and you have your stubbornness from your false mind or false conception of what you think you should be. When people hold such a mind, there is always conflict. People do not truly accept each other.

The achieved one's best actions come from his spiritual nature which is as eternal as the universal moral law. "I am not going to please you, I am going to do what is right for this situation according to the nature of the universe." He makes his decisions clearly, not for the reason that he is your father, or that someone has done him a special favor, but because there is a universal law, a universal morality. In important matters, a person cannot do things that would be harmful to others or oneself just to try to please somebody.

Suppose your brother is involved with gangsters. You cannot say, "I must help him or go with him to do what he likes because he is my brother." This is similar to trying to please someone. If you wish to advance yourself spiritually, you would rather like to stop the evil growth of your brother.

In every situation, everybody wishes that others agree with them. It is not necessary. We need to do what is right for the situation, not just do what I think is right or you think is right. This is what we call universal righteousness.

If everybody looked for great truth as I describe it, there would be no contention in the world, only enjoyment. There would be no fighting, only looking for what is right.

Q: We have the small mind, the limited mind; there is also the big mind, the universal mind. What is the source of the universal mind?

Master Ni: Universal mind is not installed or already inside of each person. It is a development. Universal nature or spiritual nature is not something that you learn from outside. Its source is inside you. You develop it from inside out. It is the original spiritual nature.

What you normally think and do, however, is what you learn from external experience in general. When you are not developed, you follow the established mind which is continually formed by your life experiences. If you continue to follow only your knowledge that comes from your limited experiences, you will turn out to be cruel, because life experiences are so rough. Roughness is not one's own nature.

Let us say you are a lady of thirty. You feel unhappy because your mom wanted you to marry a doctor and so far you have not achieved that goal. But according to your original nature, the nature of the universe, who is right for you to marry? There is not even such a requirement as marriage by the universe; people are generally pushed by custom.

The real source and joy of life is original existence. It is only the falseness of the mind which brings about trouble. For forty years now, following the Second World War, there has been strong contention between the superpowers of Russia and America. Will this last forever? No, it cannot. Many people died in the 40 years of struggle. Great tension and nervous conditions were brought to the people of those two countries. But tension and nervousness do not have to be the way for people to live their lives.

I know my practice. Although spiritual energy is formless and traceless, it has a little tendency that can be seen. It is light, whole and independent, and does not bother. So my wish to attain Tao is to maintain the lightness, purity, wholeness and integrity of my spiritual nature. My spiritual nature has no form, but my lightness can be formed. Clearness can be traced; therefore, by practicing clearness, I live with my spiritual nature. Whenever a life situation or experience causes me to lose my clearness, my wholeness of spirit, or the unity or peace within, I consider that the experience is not worth further consideration, because of my spiritual awareness. I consider that anything that disturbs me and goes against my inner harmony is not worth seeing or doing at all.

We are forced, in different situations, to talk and do things. Such is the necessity of the world, but in reality any fight, disagreement or argument does not exist. It is only created or brought about in a situation. How do we avoid such conflict? Two achieved spiritual persons do not need to fight with their mind or disposition; they only lay the facts out on the table. They review the facts to find the best solution for the trouble.

A person who does not see there is no need for competition or conflict only looks for favor from others. Why should anyone consider giving favor to another? A favor-seeker thinks too much for himself; the result is trouble for himself. He thinks too much for himself because he has nervous tension from his life experience, and always wishes to take something.

Once I described that the roosters in the farmland search each minute for food. They cannot stop. It is their tendency. In humans, this tendency is false mind. If people could stop doing that for one or two hours, and say, "I am not starving, my life is not finished," and do something else for a while, maybe they would live longer. To have a long life is not the nature of chickens. For higher, more evolved life beings, there is a possibility of seeing the source or deep root of spiritual nature. When we live close to the spiritual nature, we will live less on the surface of the world's struggle.

So now you can understand the two parts: being yourself with your spiritual nature or being somebody else you imagine you would like to be.

The first part is a life in which you do not need to struggle for gain. How great a life it is; the experience of a six-month old child is to have full energy for itself, and experience only joy after eating or after elimination.

The second part is like being someone or something else, such as an all-time winner. There is always some conflict or disagreement there, or some effort which needs to be made. You made more effort for extra gain to your true nature; thus, you have missed the side of being yourself, which is always light, clear, natural, joyful and organic. The side of false mind is hard work and a hard fight. Many people, as adults, eat and eliminate, but are still unhappy. We still have the opportunity, if we live with the wholeness of spirit, to be ourselves and to be happy. But most of the time we pull our attention away from being ourselves, to do something different. Thus, whenever we do something, we find it does not always go smoothly.

From which part do you gain more? You gain more from the part from which you do not need to make an effort, struggle or reach for agreement. The agreement is there. But people are foolish; rather than living that way, they are only looking to see what they can win from a fight. The excitement and stimulation from fighting is not peace. Clearness or clarity, however, is a much better achievement than anything you can win by fighting. If you do not think that clarity is achievement, you will find no reward in spiritual practice.

So even though you struggle during your life, how much money can you make? How high a position can you have? You can expand your personal ego over anybody, but finally you will see that ego is empty, void and untruthful. Why extend your ego over somebody by conquering? If you can conquer other people, what is the true attainment you can get? A false sense of glory is what you use to cheat yourself. By conquering, you create struggle. Through struggling or conquering, you may achieve your purpose, but then again, maybe not. Pain and disappointment in being unable to achieve your purpose may already be installed.

Let us say, for example, that you experience joy, excitement and rejoicing because you have achieved your purpose of extending your personal ego and have won a disagreement. You are successful in conquering other people. What is the fun of it? It is only on the emotional level. In emotion, you feel one moment a little delight because your ego is swelling, but then, after that, there is only emptiness. In the natural world, however, nobody is better and nobody is less than anybody else. People do not recognize it because of their education and the false concept of self.

The great leaders once hailed, "Long live somebody." The people once hailed, "Long live the king." But can they live long? People struggle for a voice to praise somebody, but that does not last long, either. In the world of daily life where money is made, it is not the part of struggle or gain that is most enjoyable. What brings enjoyment and delight is eternal peace; that which is of eternity, eternal wholeness, eternal organic condition of life, mind and spirit! That is the real reward. That is the real enjoyment.

Visitor: Master Ni, I will carve your teaching on my bone!

Master Ni: Better to eat it and chew it.

INNER LIGHT

Visitor: I would like to have a poised mind and soul. Please teach me how.

Master Ni: All right, I will suggest several principles that can help your mind stay poised, correctly functioning and ready to respond well in all situations. At times, not being poised could present a potentially fatal situation to an individual. It is impossible for a person to always avoid the rise of a habitual group of thoughts or emotional patterns from arising in certain circumstances. However, it is possible and necessary to learn the poised mind. This is the same sort of training one receives from external, physical learning of Tao Chi Ch'uan movement, which helps one attain internal and external poise at any time and in any position. Attaining a poised mind is a spiritual practice rather than a psychological program.

First, the mind must, in any situation, be neutral. This is the first direct way to obtain and be with a poised mind.

Second, the mind needs always to be poised between the innermost consciousness and the conscience during all external pulls, or the gradual or sudden collapse of the pulls.

Third, maintain flexibility. By being flexible, one attains the poised mind. Flexibility means that a person's mind cannot become fossilized or rigid by the information and knowledge to which one is exposed or pulled. It means that a person does not adhere to different items of information, or anything else that he has contacted or gathered. He is not bound by his preferences. Rigidity and preference create bad companies, bad dynasties and bad governments. In the Taoist classics there is much talk about government; they are talking figuratively about the human mind. Both work in the same way.

It is interesting that our forerunners, the naturally developed Taoists, treated or considered the mind as energy. When this energy is full, healthy and natural, it usually serves a person better and rewards him more. He gets more from its use; it gives accuracy and exactness in its service. However, when a person indulges in uncritical listening to the historical "big names" or established images of authority with their good and bad influences, and fails to apply centeredness and nurture the pure subtle energy which is the real mind itself, then not only is his behavior wrong but his whole life is in trouble. If a person is in an important position in his society, he can become sick or dangerous by not applying centeredness and nurturing the pure subtle energy.

Before you apply a unit of energy in the mind by using it as information or by transforming it into thoughts or emotion, that pure energy is called spirit or mental essence or, in Chinese, sen. Sen means spirit, pure spirit. It is true spirit. By nurturing this pure spirit, you can produce new clarity. Clarity is the highest kind of spirit. The highest spiritual energy is called ming or crystal clarity. It is not self-deceiving. It is not deceived by information or knowledge, either internal or external. How can you achieve it? To achieve ming, you gather external information by listening to talks and reading books, but you also need to work on it: you nurture the pure chi, the pure spirit, the simple mind. It is not the same as working on an emotional state or a concept.

Before energy is formalized, it is natural energy, subtle as a warm snowflake. Most people are unaware of its existence. It is spirit. Ordinary people, in practicing their cultivation, believe that to sit in meditation is still to be involved in thinking. Thoughts are always affected by your knowledge-condition, life experiences and your teachers. These could make you dependent, make you a slave; that dependency might misguide and mislead you. So there comes a time when you cannot use the intellectual teachings any more. The most important guidance for any student is: directly reach the spiritual energy above the center of the mind and grow and increase the ming, the light.

Ming is light. Clarity is light. Without this light, you cannot achieve clarity and you cannot see anything as it really is.

Beginning in infancy, the senses start to grow and they continually stimulate the evolution of the mind. Then through different learning processes, the mind gathers more information. However, it may be a collection of junk or some mixture of helpful and harmful knowledge. If you do not develop your internal light, even a little bit, then what you follow in your life is what other people have already fashioned for you. That is social custom; it is what people do. Perhaps it is what your parents have told you to do. But if you follow the code of social custom, you can never go beyond what you have been given.

In universal human society, sometimes a breakthrough is made in all spheres. A new solution or helpful contribution is brought about by a person whose life proceeds from the natural essence. He has manifested his inner light. This inner light can be nurtured. This inner light is God, which is, of course, not the description given in the religious books, because the books tell about the dead god, not the living god. The alive god is within; it is the inner light. The inner light is nurtured and supported by spirit. Spiritual essence is an evolution from the mind and mind is an evolution from the essence of the body. If you do not nurturing your physical energy to support your mind, your mind is unable to mature.

For example, if you use your energy on sex and you overdo it, your mind will be damaged. Your thinking system slows down and you make mistakes. You cannot handle driving a car. It is similar to being drunk. Excess alcohol also damages the mind, temporarily and permanently, and the person who overindulges makes mistakes.

The physical universe is the foundation of spiritual growth. High spirits and light are the basic stuff of universal nature. Only if you raise yourself to a certain vibration can you achieve universal spirit, which is also called the subtle light of the universe. The subtle light of the universe has no words to describe it; it is not east, west, north or south; it is not man or woman; it is not today, tomorrow or yesterday. This universal light can be applied at any time. This is the center of internal cultivation; the center brings achievement.

You fear yourself when your physical energy is low. Too much emotion or worry masks the light and does not allow you to say, "I need to be gentle." It is gentleness that keeps away disturbances of all sorts, such as emotions and conceptual knowledge. Just by embracing and nurturing the purity and clarity of divine light, you will be achieved. You are not less than the sages of any time or place.

All spiritual leaders formalize an intention to respond to the demands and circumstances of the times. They have better minds because they have worked perseveringly to develop them. They refer to the better mind as god. You have that kind of mind too, but perhaps you have not yet developed it enough. However, using one's mind with an intention to influence people is not always correct because it is activated by a reaction to a circumstance. That is one use of the mind. It is sometimes helpful on a certain level; we are speaking of something still higher than that.

The most valuable human activity is to nurture the divine light of nature, of agelessness, timelessness, of no place or gender discrimination. That is our true life. It is life. Many times I mention physical or low level spirit; this spirit is individual. At the high, subtle level, spirit is universal. Only your gentleness, delicacy and subtlety can allow you to reach and nurture that high light within you. Intensify your light, at least in your cultivation, sufficiently to illuminate the steps of your forward progress.

Your question concerns the soul. The soul is a part of life, associated with the mind, past experience, past ego and past emotion. You now receive a new opportunity to be further evolved and to go beyond the patterns of the past. If you are driven by the old soul, then old mistakes, old life conditions and old patterns of emotion, not only from one lifetime but from ten or a hundred lifetimes, will keep you at a low level. In that case, you are not achieved and not evolving. Rather than being a matter of saving the soul; your spiritual evolution is a matter of nurturing the soul; evolving, educating, cultivating and developing it.

Popular or general religion tends to concern itself with saving the soul. They conceive of an old soul as dying, no longer a growing, progressing soul. That is a psychological attitude; the reality is they do not save any souls at all. Religion offers quicksand into which souls looking for comfort only sink.

Everybody has a soul. Attaining the soul's growth is not a matter of protecting the soul. It is a matter of developing and educating the soul to evolve into a high personal soul. Once the personal soul is evolved, then the mental spirit, the mind, becomes identified with the new life of your new soul, a new unity in the universe which cannot be extinguished. The natural opportunity to do that is given equally to everybody, but human life expresses itself in different strengths.

Let us talk about a person as having two aspects, physical and spiritual. These two aspects combine to make a human life. Many other lives, such as the more developed animals and the less developed people, are also natural, but they are not positioned for the highest spiritual evolution.

With a great opportunity for growth at hand, what are you looking for? A person who still looks to his undeveloped past evidently still needs to preserve the old soul of backwardness and mistakes. Such a person will not receive salvation; he will receive downfall. A wise person can immediately recognize the right instruction about how to practice, how to protect himself, how to grow and how to make himself strong. This is the essence of this teaching. Practice, protection, growth and strength are the purpose of the two spheres in joining together. This is what we teach in this tradition.

Q: How does the soul evolve? What is its relationship with all the other parts of me: body, mind and spirit?

Master Ni: This is a basic question. We have already talked about it many times. There are three sources of the soul, the three dan tien. The lower dan tien is the physical center, the reproductive or sexual energy level. The middle dan tien, at the point between the nipples, is the center of the mind, or energy of the chi level. The brain center is the point between the eyebrows, the upper dan tien, where a person refines his spiritual energy.

So there are basically three centers, three different authorities. Through making a basic, systematic examination of the decisions you make, the words you speak and the thoughts you think, you can tell which one has the strongest influence in your life.

We have these three partners in life. The partner at the lower dan tien is the center of vitality; it is most interested in material and sexual enjoyment. The next partner is the middle sphere of life at the level of the mind. It originates and transforms all kinds of interests and desires and, with the training of the mind, it can become aware of the necessity of looking for balance. The achievement of balance still depends on the influence and training that the mind has experienced. The highest partner is one's spirit, residing in the upper dan tien. It has its own tendency, interest and behavior coming from the spiritual level, and, if it is expressed, is always giving, yielding and kind. Sometimes it might cause a costly and ineffective decision in life if not balanced by the other partners.

At night, the soul sinks down to the lower part of the body. In the morning it ascends to the brain again; otherwise, the mind does not wake up. Consider that there is not only one soul, but several, as representatives of different places in the being. They all meet together in the mind, conjointly making a decision or formulating an approach or resolving to yield to something. It is also true that there are different energy contributions to the body; the different strengths of a person constitute his different attitudes toward life.

Taoists talk about three centers of energy and some other traditions talk about there being seven chakras; in reality there are many more than these. For example, in the head area alone there are from seven to nine; more evolved people have more partners or energy centers. They are not the main partners of your life because at the spiritual level, it is the different varieties of energy that make your spirit strong.

I would like to tell you more about the soul. One's ancestors still live in one's body. Once a person dies, his life energy returns to the next generation and this continues with the following generations. A descendant receives these souls or life forces as parasites; they dwell in the back of the head, near the base of the brain.

Q: As parasites? Do you mean that they drain my energy instead of adding to it?

Master Ni: That depends.

Also, when you study the work of an achieved mind, the thoughts produced by your efforts are of a similar level as the material you work on. By experiencing the same vibration, you have reached the teaching and now that teacher's energy resides on the top part of your head. That is to say, the thoughts related to the studying that you have done resonate at a certain vibration similar to that achieved by the person who did the writing. By studying their material, the energy of the teachers' achievement also comes to join the top part of your head.

When you have sex with different partners, depending on the situation, you gather or lose some energy and the other person does too.

Each day our energy is transforming, gathering, scattering and reorganizing; it keeps doing that. There are only a few main centers, like a battery or a generator that produces the energy. You are a generator; you can gather, receive and transmit. This is why our tradition of spiritual cultivation says be poised, be centered, be neutral, be pure, be natural. If you follow this way of spiritual cultivation, you are growing, you are progressing. Energy, especially at the high attainment, only reaches its same high radiating level. If your thinking is good and your speaking is good and your doing is good, you always gather or attract beneficial spiritual energy. If your thinking is bad and your actions are bad, you can gather energy only at that level.

Human people have a lot of freedom to go upward or downward; the direction of the movement depends on the evolution of one's soul. Your question practically says, "Am I one, three or seven?" I think you are many. I am many. But, with many spirits, are you unified? That is important. If you have a unified soul, you are achieved. If you are distorted and have disharmonious and disintegrated souls, then you are involved in a struggle. In one part of you, you would like to do one thing but you hear another subtle voice saying you would like to do something else. By engaging in this tug of war, your internal energy keeps pulling you from your goal. All your energy is expressing, instead, the sickness of your mind, your body and your spirit. Attainment is being able to be fully in the present moment.

The symbol of achievement is one, unity, wholeness. It is not saying, I am seven or I am a hundred. In Taoism, we say that there are 36,000 spirits that compose a person. Any small problem that causes disunification means trouble. Once unified, there is peace. When you do things and you are integrated, you express a unified, harmonious, singular projection of total energy. You are one united expression. The importance of cultivation is expressed clearly in the *Tao Teh Ching*. Cultivation is to embrace oneness. If you have any thoughts that propagate divergence, you are hearing a new projection. Cultivation saves your soul from doing multiplication. Multiplication is the act of self-dividing your own spirit, or not organizing your spirits into a harmonious unity.

So the direction of cultivation is clear: attaining one is the goal. Embracing one is the means. Reaching the one is the purpose. Life is integration. Death is disintegration. What I tell you is the truth.

A god is the integration of good energy. A devil is the integration of bad energy. A human can be either godly or devilish. Between evolution and devolution, healthy energy can always be reached. If you move from a place of devolution to one of evolution in your personal growth, you can reach a place of healthy energy if you are wise enough to avoid temporary, selfish, narrow interests. Yes, you can attain your personal interests, but not by using harmful means to achieve them. Each person, in the universal sense, is a part of you.

So now you can be happy. You have learned the way to organize and unify yourself with your source. Do not let yourself become emotional, melancholy or saddened. Have the goal of being unified. How can you be unified? Be poised, centered, neutral, strong and pure. That is all there is to it. The cultivation is the same for everyone; however, religions usually have a different purpose that is more of a literary character than the realistic spiritual sciences.

Q: It seems that a person cannot always stay neutral or centered, often for reasons beyond his or her control.

Master Ni: You are pulled by your physics. Women have a menstruation cycle which pulls their energy down. Do not be bothered by that. Nobody is always down. Natural life, emotionally, psychologically and spiritually, has an up and down rhythm. It is up to you to decide the character of the rhythm; in most people, the curve may be very steep and not graceful; it can be confused. Through spiritual achievement you find constancy, a beautiful rhythm, as in a piece of music. A good piece of music is not always high notes or low notes. Beautiful music consists of an arrangement of notes of many different pitches, all harmoniously arranged or organized. Life itself is the music of energy organization or the musical organization of energy.

Do not worry. When you feel melancholy, look at it and say, "Ah! This is something like singing the blues." When your energy starts to become cheerful, you might say, "How beautiful." It is the variety of notes that makes the music of life beautiful. That is the art and we need to achieve it. We need not be discouraged by the voice of the low notes, because they are also a part of the self. Everything in the universe is composed of beautiful music, even the wordless, soundless positive power.

WHEN SAGES STOP TEACHING, PEOPLE CAN BE CONFUSED AND LOST

Master Ni's Talk at the Chinese Community Center, Atlanta, Georgia, February 18, 1989

I

Thank you, Professor Chien, for introducing me to all of you here today as the Master of Tao. But you know, among Chinese people I am not renowned. Heavenly Master Tsang, for example, who did the service of exorcism among villagers, was even supported by the emperors of the late generation. My practice is different; it is the pure teaching of Tao, which comes from the *I Ching* or *Book of Changes.* That is the center of my teaching. The goal of my practice is the union of Tao and people, just like the marriage between a man and woman. We do the spiritual practice of Tao. In ordinary language, the joining of the nature and the person in your life-being is the goal of our practice and teaching.

Nature is human; human is nature. If any separation is caused, it is because humans lose their vision and cannot see the truth of life. We live in human society; we are conditioned in an artificial culture with multiple creations of concepts. We need to respond to all the artificial cultural demands and commands, so we become artificial. People are students of artificial religions and cultures and they lose their own connection with the true being of natural life. There is nothing strange about one's true being; it is so simple. It is nothing beyond your life. However, misguided people who are lost in the ocean of artificial mist and pollution cannot see their true selves any more.

This path is originally from an ancient time before any artificial religion and culture were created. My tradition and I are not as popular as the worldly religions. The first discipline for us is not to look for popularity, but to do the service at all right occasions without neglecting to realize the truth, the integral truth, in our lives. Perhaps you wondered about what a heavenly master is after hearing about my background. My teaching continues the tradition from Tien Tai mountain which is located in southeastern Chikiang province. Tien Tai mountain means "the mountain of heavenly terrace." It is a Taoist mountain. It has eight peaks surrounding the central peak, which is called the lotus peak. It is also considered to be shaped as the set of hexagrams that form an octagon like the diagram of the Tai Chi Ba Gua. In the early Chan Dynasty, a prince cultivated himself there on that mountain and became achieved. This is a short poem that describes him:

> *"The young prince went to the mountain*
> *to look for the immortal teacher.*
> *Finally he achieved his immortality*
> *which can help him reach the highest Heaven.*
>
> *However, if one stays in such an immortal cave*
> *for just seven days,*
> *In the world, there has already passed*
> *a solid thousand years."*

Later, in the Jing Dynasty, Go Hong also cultivated himself in the mountain center. Master Go Hong specialized in internal alchemy. His book is titled *Bao Po Tzu,* which is the name for one who embraces the simple essence. The word "cultivation" is the popular term for Taoists who consider that the natural essence inside and outside of physical life can sustain people's lives and make them durable and capable. They cultivate or grow this natural essence. With this purpose, this action of cultivation can also be described as "refining one's immortal medicine," and a number of achieved Taoists refined their immortal medicine there in that mountain.

During the Tang dynasty,[1] there was a famous heavenly master called Su Ma Chen Jing. Su Ma Chen Jing specialized in setting steps for Taoist cultivation and meditation with the purpose of gradually controlling personal internal and external energy. This master received his title as the Heavenly Teacher from the emperor of the dynasty. He continued the teaching from Go Hong to Dao Fung Jing. Master Dao Fung Jing was a Taoist who lived in the mountains. He was renowned by being the number one advisor to the Liang Dynasty.[2] He was influential to the emperor while he remained as a hermit. He specialized in discerning natural spiritual energy and Chinese herbal medicine. If you read his biography, you can see his political or cultural influence. He was mainly active in Mou Mountain of Jiang Su, north of Tien Tai. Mou mountain later became the center of Taoist culture, and later, Tien Tai became the center of Taoism and Buddhism.

From those mountains, Taoists developed themselves mostly in the arts of medicine and spiritual power. The Heavenly Master Su Ma Chen Jing continued Dao Fung Jing's tradition on Tien Tai mountain. Later, during the Sung dynasty, Master Chiang Tzu Yang was the successor of the teaching in cultivating golden immortal medicine. Chiang Tzu Yang specialized in beneficial sex for spiritual purpose. He was a native of Tien Tai and also gave his important teaching there.

In the practice of golden immortal medicine, the school of Tsang Tzu Yang is usually considered as a southern school. The northern school engages in a social or religious movement. They live in Taoist monasteries or nunneries as an ascetic practice of life. They wear uniforms, and have a certain hairstyle and ritual. They depend on donations from society and the support of the monarch. The northern school does not approve of sexual life but makes being a Taoist as an occupation. The north developed as a religion

---

[1] 618-906 A.D.

[2] 502-556 A.D.

which promotes a single practice. It has a shorter history. The southern school are people who stay in ordinary life, which is more adaptable. Basically, the teaching of the Southern and Northern schools is the same. A student of Tao is open to learning from both of them. As to how to organize one's life and one's teaching, this is still one's individual style. I affirm the scientific attitude of the south, although it is not necessarily my own practice in the areas that are too special. There are still later developed schools of west and east. Three of the schools, south, west and east, are usually personal practice and continue the Taoist knowledge of beneficial sexual activity with some extent of Taoist dual cultivation. Among all four, the south was the original. The initiating master is Lu, Tung Ping.

The spiritual attitude of most Taoists in the later generations is integral. A Taoist may be a Buddhist but does not abandon the world. He may be a Confucianist but does not serve the monarch. He may be a practitioner of Zahn (Zen) but does not stay in a monastery. In more modern times, he also could be a Christian, but does not belong to any church. He may be a member of Judaism but it does not mean he cannot have his personal spiritual growth. He may be a Moslem but he does not trust that any war is holy. He may be a communist but is still open to the study of truthful spiritual reality. Basically, he is a Taoist; he likes to be original and natural, above all. He is religious but is not bound by any religion. Yet he does not fight with any religion or customs. None of them becomes his special adhesive.

Our attitude is a little different from teaching Taoism as an occupation or as a custom of an old society. Being a Taoist student is an achievement, not a custom. Each person has the responsibility to refresh himself in a new time to attain the important achievement spiritually, physically and mentally. From the integral truth one becomes an integral being with the universal integral oneness.

Tien Tai mountain is beautiful. Many years ago two woodcutters, Lu and Roan, entered the mountain and lost their way. Neither of them knew the way out, but they suddenly discovered in the nearby stream, a petal from a peach flower. So they followed the stream, and soon they discovered two young girls playing. They asked directions from the girls and made their acquaintance. They treated each other kindly and not long after the men married the girls. They enjoyed the most beautiful life there on the mountain. Lu and Roan enjoyed themselves tremendously with all kinds of natural food and natural pleasure.

But they were humans who had the habit of human life, and one day they missed their home. They said, "We miss our home, so we will go for a visit and then come back." Their wives agreed to let them go. Lu and Roan found their way back to their village by following the stream, but when they arrived there, nothing was familiar to them. They asked the local people, who were wearing different clothing from that of their old village, for their family and friends. No one in the village could tell them anything. The two woodcutters became quite confused. "Just a few days ago, we entered the mountain, now we are back, but why are things so strange?" After many inquiries and difficulties, they found somebody very old in the village who told them, "When I was a young child, my grandpa told me a story of two woodcutters who went into the mountain and never came back." That was the answer. They did not know that they had already become natural immortals. They just did not know. So now, despite the hospitality that the villagers showed them, they were no longer used to human life, and went back to the mountain.

When I was young, I was interested in this story. Rather than go through all the trouble of cultivation, I just wanted to meet a girl like Lu and Roan married in order to save lots of time and hard work in achieving my immortality. But my destiny was hard work, a long time of cultivation, and learning about my tradition.

Now I am an American. When I was interviewed in the naturalization office, the officer, who was a woman, asked me to give up my title, saying that American citizens cannot have any title. I said, "This is neither a title given by authority of society nor a social position in which people recognize me. It is a somewhat different teaching that instructs people not to put their life energy into something like seeking titles. The word 'Taoist' goes before the word 'master.' It is a respectful form of address, just like 'madame,' etc. The words 'Taoist Master' describe a reality of a way of life characterized by natural living and enjoying one's own life energy. If a person likes titles, that is a sign of his undevelopment." It seems that the officer did not understand about the Taoist way of life. She thought a Taoist master is something like a duke or a person of similar title from the European countries. Anyway, she let me pass through naturalization, and I am still an untitled citizen of the universe spiritually. A Taoist maintains his freedom from any social title unless he sincerely decides to play the game as the title defines. People of Tao respect the untitled, not the titled. Most people respect the titles.

Many Chinese now come to the United States to teach Taoism. This is encouraging. Yet to call themselves masters is not necessary, because even a real spiritual background or traditional connection does not mean much to modern life. I think it is agreeable for social custom. Perhaps young teachers use it to establish a business. However, it does not prove any authority. An achieved one is ashamed to utilize any title to establish a position among people without the natural process of letting people recognize what he or she is. The true masters are those who harmoniously live a good life and enjoy it. A teacher of Tao has great interest in improving himself. The purpose of his teaching is to transfer the benefit of spiritual cultivation to others.

We value the learning, achievement and knowledge that came from the time earlier than Fu Shi. Fu Shi was the one who gathered all the important information from our much earlier human ancestors. He first developed symbols; not written words, but a system of symbols. Historically, we could say that ancient human culture arose at the time those symbols began to be used. They later evolved into words. At least, his symbols were the first system used to describe philosophy developed by the ancients. At its beginning, *The Book of Changes* had no words, only the symbols developed by Fu Shi, yet it contained all the information and all the inspiration from nature compiled through generations.

Far later than the origin of the *Book of Changes* in China, there was the attraction of different religions in general society: Confucianism, Buddhism and folk Taoism, the latter being a combination of the main religions. Though these three religions became active and popular, the *Book of Changes* still retains its superior position in describing the truth of human life and the nature of the universe.

Today, the descendants of the ancient Chinese do not have much to be proud of. There is, of course, the teaching of the *Book of Changes*. This book expresses the essence of early human spiritual achievement.

II

Q: What is Tao?

Master Ni: Tao is the soul of Chinese culture. All of you here know that you are the descendants of the Yellow Emperor, who lived only around 5,000 years ago. But you do not know about the people born before the Yellow Emperor's time. If we trace back to before his time, do you know who were your great-great grandfathers and great-great grandmothers? Who were your earlier ancestors? Would you like to know who they were? There is an answer.

There is a mountain named Tai Mountain, the great mountain, in San Kung province. Confucius was born in that province around 2,500 years ago. It was ancient custom in all early generations for each new emperor or king, when first taking the reins of China, to go to Tai Mountain and worship Heaven. This custom was followed before written history. Also it was a custom that when the new rulers went to Tai Mountain to make a sacrifice or offering, they carved their names in the stones. It is similar to what we often see in some scenic spot or tourist site in the United States; people carve their names in the stones or on the bark of trees. That is a human habitual tendency. It is similar to wolves or dogs marking their territory as a natural tendency or low instinct. Our ancestors had the same kind of habit.

It is fortunate that they had that habit and carved their name in the stones. In the epoch of Spring and Autumn, which lasted from approximately 722-484 B.C., a group of scholars went to Tai Mountain to check out the names and dynasties. They wanted to know how many people were leaders in the different ancient generations. They developed a search of the ancient record.

What they discovered was that at the least, just the name was given. In ancient times, you see, because there was no written language, each generation's emperor had a special picture or symbol. So they ascertained from the symbols of the leaders of different generations, that up to their time in the Epoch of Spring and Autumn, 2,700,000 years had passed since this custom started. From the number of years, they determined that there were seventy-two families. Each family started a dynasty and their descendants continued it. When one dynasty finished, a new dynasty began. Before the Yellow Emperor, who lived around 5,000 years ago, seventy-two families meant seventy-two dynasties. The scholars divided these seventy-two dynasties into ten periods of time.

The question you asked me is about Tao. So now I will give you the answer. What is called Tao is the experience, essence, knowledge and achievement of over 2,700,000 years of all the dynasties, if any. Perhaps you call it wisdom. Humans had been in all kinds of situations and learned the most truthful, reliable knowledge of all. They learned the position of human life in the universe and so forth. In totality, it is an accumulation of knowledge and achievement from when the ancestors faced different challenges in their lives. I may say the accumulation and achievement from that length of time is Tao. Tao is not a knowledge or philosophy that has been accomplished. Tao is not dying, Tao is continuing. Someone might ask, "What about Lao Tzu, who said, 'The Tao that can be expressed is not the true Tao?'" I think it is answered by Lao Tzu. He did not attempt to define the truth. He described the nature of truth.

From generation to generation, our human ancestors faced different challenges. They find their way or a principle to handle problems. Once they find an effective solution, then that unchangeable, unbreakable, invaluable, indestructible truth is recognized as Tao. We say Tao is the way of life. Tao is the way of eternal life. It is not partial life, only a certain section, or a partial experience that can be produced. Therefore, Tao is not an individual personal creation. It is wisdom derived from numberless generations so far.

It was clear at the time of Confucius, around 2,500 years ago, that there was disorder in society. The world had changed to a new phase which presented the downfall of the ancient spiritual culture with its long lasting harmony. People were developing differently: they were developing intellectually. They were looking for personal expansion instead of the guidance of Tao; the entire society of ancient China was thrown into turmoil. At that time, three masters came to respond. One I have already mentioned is Confucius. The others are Mo Tzu and Lao Tzu. Lao Tzu is much older than the other two, and perhaps it was his more advanced age that gave him a deeper wisdom to respond to the new situation. Some people say that Taoist teaching came after Confucius; they think that Lao Tzu must be younger than Confucius, but that is wrong.

So at that time in human history, suddenly people changed. All sages sensed that there were no more responsible leaders or kings, there were no more responsible descendants or children. People did not take responsibility for anything anymore; they just did what they liked. So the world became confused. To use Confucius' language: "It is a time when a king is not a king and a minister is not a minister. A father is not a father, and a son is not a son. Then, what are they? They are robbers and troublemakers." These three sages say, "We have Tao; we do not need to be confused." These three teachers present a different understanding of the ancient Tao. Each wished to guide people back to Tao. So one teacher promoted being kind and proper. Another teacher promoted universal love. Another teacher promoted doing nothing against your original nature.

All people do something. If you have something to do and it is visible, becomes famous, makes you rich, or is recognized or regarded by the public as either good or bad, this means you must have done something against your nature. That means you have done something against Tao. The principle of wu wei, doing nothing extra, is not to say a person stays there doing nothing; it means he does all the things necessary for him to do, but nothing against his own nature. Nor does wu wei mean something like a description of typical modern life where people are so busy, rushing around, doing this and that, looking for interesting or fun things. How much do those activities really relate to our life nature? Mostly they are responses to artificial social commands.

In other words, what does it mean not to do anything against your nature? What is nature? A fish, for example, can live in water. Fish are happy in water. If the fish jumps on the shore, can it enjoy living in the air or lying on the dry land? Another example is ants. They are so faithful in their life and active everywhere. That is their nature. Can you put ants in water? No, they will not live. In our human lives, our behavior and decisions of whether to proceed or retreat from an action or situation should not follow the dictates of our personal likes and dislikes, as the world tells us. We must look to our nature to see what is right. If natural virtue prevails among people, we can go ahead to live and work with them. If natural virtue is obstructed by people themselves, then we need to retreat. If something we do damages the generally good organic condition of other people or society, but is not imposed by social force, it should not be done again. Any teaching that is truly serviceable to your life must not be against your true life nature. The three sages offered their teaching 2,500 years ago. The trouble of human society has not been resolved. The bad situation has been continued by all generations. Although there have been some good periods, the basic trend has not changed. But the modern world is different and teaches otherwise.

In later human culture, religions and politics developed a manipulative and confusing language. Their language was designed to make lies sound truthful and murder respectable. In democratic countries, politicians with their skillful language sometimes give an appearance of solidity to pure wind. In the modern Chinese community, Chinese communism changes white to black and black to white; many people fall into a power struggle with their leaders. In school, children are taught, "I don't love my father and mother, I love the Communist Party." That is against the life nature. It is clearly a bad example of twisted human culture, similar to most religions and political parties.

My answer to your question of what is Tao is: whatever benefits your spirit and your life is Tao. Whatever does not really serve your life, but pulls your life away to sacrifice for a certain purpose, is not Tao. The cultural essence of China is the chung. Chung means the center. The ancient symbol for chung is " **⊕**," which portrays an arrow in the center of a bow. It is the most rightful place for the arrow to be. Later, it was written as " ⊕ " for easy writing, but it means the same. Chung, or centeredness, means arriving at the right point, not overdoing something and not lacking something. In other words, chung means appropriateness. What is good and what is bad? If we use the standard of chung or appropriateness to judge something, then whatever is too much or not enough is bad, and whatever hits the mark is good.

Sometimes chung is mistranslated as middle way. It can be the middle point but not the middle way. I would rather avoid using the word middle, and use 'right point' or 'properness.'

Let us use Tai Chi Ch'uan exercise to illustrate the principle of chung or being centered. When in Tai Chi practice you utilize your strength, you must always be centered and able to keep your balance. If you over-use your strength, you have already lost your balance, then if you add even a little bit of strength to the direction in which you are going, certainly you will fall over. To practice Tai

Chi movement is to learn how to make all movements properly and correctly from one's own supportive and reliable position. It is not to look for an opportunity to conquer others. It is not to be forceful or fierce looking or aggressive. The secret of winning depends on your correct movement. Tai Chi Ch'uan practice is not meant to practice for a fight; it is the training of the principle of properness in all ordinary life. In life or in Tai Chi practice, following those principles means that rather than fight, you give yourself tremendous room and freedom in movement.

All of this means that in our lives, we may enjoy doing something or may like to become rich. However, if our behavior and cultivation are not right, enjoyment and wealth become burdens to us and eventually end up harming us through overindulgence and emotion. There is a principle that says, It does not matter whether you move or keep still; either way, do not lose your center point.

What is Tao? I am talking about Tao. Once you learn this, you know how to manage your life and you attain Tao. What else? Many people would like to attain health, to be happy and live long, but they do something that upsets the reality behind this principle, and then their purpose cannot be achieved. Instead, their behavior makes them troubled, and then they suffer more than if they hadn't done anything! The principle of harmony or appropriateness cannot be changed. Such truth as the principle of life is unshakable. All people know it, but few people can do it. People would rather follow the secondary teaching of religions. Only a few can conform to the high principles in everyday life.

Q: To me, the religion of Tao is mysterious. My knowledge about Tao comes from reading different novels. Those marvelous Chinese novels make me really wonder. Some say that once a Taoist is in meditation, his own spirit will go out. Is this something unnatural? I am more familiar with Buddhism and have not read anything like that in the Buddhist texts.

Master Ni: I would like to answer your question, but I do not wish to confuse you. What you described is not the experience of the novel writers. It is the experience of those who stay in the mountains. They concentrate their energy to project their spiritual power or conscious power to any subject, object or matter they wish to know. It is possible, but it is not the purpose of learning or attaining Tao. It is only one part or one proof of Taoist cultivation in a certain stage. It makes a person truly understand that life can be recreated and evolved to a higher stage of living without form. It is one thing a person who engages in Taoist cultivation can do to find a special proof for himself. Then there is much farther to go.

The main play of Taoist cultivation is energy. If one's energy is scattered, there is death. Once one's energy is gathered, it can be put into any form. In ordinary life, it would seem that there is a master or circumstance that forms the energy to be a certain shape; the big natural background forms all different kinds of life in one sphere. A Taoist does not say, "I obey, I offer my obedience absolutely to the creator (nature)." He needs to manage his own life energy, refine and transform it into whatever form or stage of life being he would like. That is freedom. It would encourage him to find a better solution to being and non-being.

Why non-being? Some spiritual traditions find that all trouble and misery come from the life of form. If there are no things, then there is no trouble, so they would rather have no life. Because they perceive that physical reality causes the trouble of life, they think that to have no physical things would bring a state of bliss; that the high spiritual promise is to be nothing, or to have a kind of emptiness devoid of form. But in Taoist cultivation, your achievement can be something, yet at the same time be nothing. You can be something and you can still be nothing. The highest freedom is the goal of your achievement. It enables you to attain the absolute, highest freedom to decide whether to be or not be, the suitability of what to be and for how long.

Because you have read some novels, you feel this description is unbelievable and strange, too far away and remote from your typical conception. In reality, Taoist practice is to totally work on one's personal energy relationship with nature and to enhance one's personal nature with the natural environment. Achieving a new stage of beingness will surely affect the world to help it transform.

It is not hard to understand that transformation happens each moment and each day. This is how a young, beautiful girl can become a mother of many children after several years. This is how a handsome young boy can grow a moustache and beard from a slippery chin. Nobody can stop transformation; it is all passive. But a Taoist converts the passive process of transformation into self-mastery. On one hand, a person who lives with obedience to the natural process is at least comparatively achieved. On the other hand, to attain self-mastery over the transforming life processes is to attain the high sphere of energy beingness.

Usually people have no freedom because they are chained in their bodies. This is why, if a person makes trouble, society can chain him or punish his body. At the same time, his soul will suffer too. Because one's soul has no freedom, the body is one's cage. However, once the highly achieved ones become achieved, the body is the garden that they can enjoy. The body is also the house. The highly achieved ones can leave it or they can live in it as they choose. There is total freedom to come and go, because they have used the body as a factory or laboratory to achieve what they would like to be. This is a totally different goal than any ordinary goal of life. An ordinary goal of life is usually social: perhaps a change from poor to rich, from a single person to the head of a big family, from a low ranking official to a leader of a country. Those are all dreams and ambitions of most people. An achieved Taoist says those are all false, because it is playing a game.

If a Taoist cannot master his soul energy or true root of life, external benefit means nothing. Taoists also live the same pattern as people leading a regular life, but they are more conscious of gathering their spiritual life. They are not totally bothered, associated or tightly linked with the emotional changes of the life pattern. Even while living an ordinary life, secretly, subtly, the Taoist is preparing his own trip to the subtle sphere. He fully utilizes the support of the lower sphere of nature, the body and the natural environment. Once he is achieved, he can choose to go at any time, either before or at the time when the physical body fails.

I do not know which Buddhist sect you belong to. The attitudes of Buddhist practice are totally different. People suffer for that. Buddhism has more literature so it is descriptive. However, the system developed by Buddhism does not eliminate the need for its followers to take care of life's troubles, although it does make it psychologically easier to accept them.

Let us say that a person has a wife who treats him badly, a family that treats him badly, a hard job and so forth. Buddhism makes him think about karma. Since it was all because of his past karma, it helps him easily tolerate the difficulties of life. This is the general Buddhist attitude. It is good, it is helpful. In the words of a metaphor of Taoism, when you cross the ocean of troubled water, no matter what method or power you use to enable yourself to cross it safely, you are the winner. So it is psychological help that enables a person to cross the ocean of troubled water, which means life.

If the wind blows against you, it provides you with an opportunity to use its strength and let it take you higher than you were before. The adversity of life can be maturation to a positive person. If one's knowledge is deep enough and the internal spirit is strong enough, one can use all kinds of situations as inspiration and a source of support for achievement. What Buddhist sect do you belong to?

III
Person: I do not belong to any religion right now, but have been reading some books about Buddhism and Taoism.

Master Ni: Chinese Buddhism is at a better cultural stage than ordinary Chinese people's belief in religious or folk

Taoism. Religious Taoism is really mixed up, with all kinds of worship. They would never dream of the high essence attained by the ancestors that I teach.

One thing you must understand is that true Buddhism, which is different than the worshipping type of Buddhism, does not worship a ghost; it worships a sage. Usually, people think that Buddha was more than a sage. They believe he was some supernatural, powerful being; sort of like God. This is a misunderstanding of general-level followers of Buddhism in China and elsewhere in Asia. In reality, Buddha's words do not present a supernatural being. He was a sage. Many ordinary people go to Buddhist temples, to worship and ask for blessings, such as to become rich, have many sons or be promoted at work. Those things are truthfully not related to Buddhist teaching. It is not true Buddhism. General Buddhism takes advantage of the average person's psychology.

Primarily, people use Buddhism for expansion of their psychological hopes, which is totally different from what developed Buddhism teaches. Alhough true Buddhism is the worship of sages, it is different from the worship of ghosts that ordinary folks worship. The difference in development is the attitude toward life.

Indian sages are different from the sages of northern Asia who developed Taoism. Some Indian sages or Jainists, who were the pioneers of Buddhism, deny any interest in worldly life. Teachers of Buddhism deny the value of life. They just wish to create something or find something as a psychological tool to diminish the pain, agony or terrible feeling in a person's mind that makes him feel he is delivered or helped by the things that give him psychological relief. It is a kind of medicine, a kind of drug; it is not reality.

True Taoism also worships sages, but those sages have a different attitude towards life. The difference is that one is open to the sunshine of life with its warmth, and the other shuts life off. Both true Taoism and true Buddhism are sage worship. What made the sages different was their attitudes of life; accordingly, their teaching varied.

The premise of Buddhism is that ordinary life is bitter. Daily life is empty; therefore, life is not worth living and a person needs to give up. Practically, who can give up life? Nobody can do it. However, at least psychologically, a person can say he is giving up life. The extreme one will stay in the monastery. The typical followers, at least when they feel troubled, just give up. This is not like the Taoist. When he faces a troubled life, he finds a way to overcome the trouble and become the winner of life. He is not stirred up by one small achievement; he keeps calm and overcomes the difficulties or troubles. He decides that this is the reality of life. Other than nurturing the strength of his spirit, there is no way he is weakened by any thought or covered by any psychological excuse.

The Buddhists decided that life, old age, sickness and dying are pain. The basic teaching is that life itself covers only four elements: being born, old, sick or dying. They decided that nobody could escape those four things, which they thought were trouble. But a spiritually achieved one thinks, "Why do they need to be trouble? They can be fun too." So, recognizing life is trouble fits the weakness of psychology. I have sympathy for those who cannot achieve themselves; they cannot find the true light in their lives. Sometimes people temporarily need a painkiller. If they do not give up on life, they can immediately look for their own spiritual strength instead of habitually utilizing a painkiller. The learning of general religion can be a process of learning Tao.

When I was a student, I was instructed to learn all the religions because the true spiritually achieved ones have no prejudice. They know that each teaching has its different function; each can serve somebody better. No single teaching can serve all people, even if it is the highest truth. Therefore, spiritual students or teachers should have no prejudice or biased insistence that only what they do is best. People have different environments, different stages of life and different growth; they need different support. In this way, all the existing teachings are spiritual riches rather than spiritual poverty of the world. Let all human beings have a chance to experience different things and attain their growth. In good time, there will be a higher light shining in their hearts.

Most of you in this group here this afternoon are interested in Tai Chi Ch'uan. There are many forms of Tai Chi Ch'uan. The form that serves your personality and stage of life is not necessarily the best for everyone. It is not true that there is only one form that is the best and all the others are useless. It is meaningless to be proud of whatever a famous teacher has taught you. It is not having a famous teacher that makes you feel good when you do Tai Chi. The way to judge a teaching or teacher is to ask if his art can serve you better. The fact that there are different forms and different schools of Tai Chi Ch'uan does not need to bother us. We first learn the foundation; then for further development, we open our minds for observation and pick up the things that can best serve our lives.

Let us talk about Chinese calligraphy as an example. Many people do calligraphy well, but all calligraphy is not the same. A person who puts energy into doing calligraphy may become recognized for his work, and then his technique becomes a school of calligraphy. But the person who is beginning to learn does not need to be bothered by the differences between the individual style of each teacher. The same is true of Tai Chi Ch'uan. Tai Chi Ch'uan can help a person, but it does not improve one's intellectual understanding or stubbornness. The real help is in the opening of his energy flow. Tai Chi Ch'uan or calligraphy are both done for the same purpose: good practice.

I need to give you an important principle. In doing any of the different practices of religion or forms of martial arts, what is important is not how high or advanced the form is; the most important thing is that you use the form to achieve yourself. Make it as a tool and use it to achieve your purpose.

I do not feel bad that so many Chinese worship Buddhism. Although it is costly and wasteful, Buddhism is still better than believing in Communism, because it has caused no violence. The main thing is that Buddhists utilize a religious form to achieve themselves, to be better persons with better understanding. Similarly, a person can utilize

Tai Chi Ch'uan or a school of calligraphy as a tool to assist the richness and abundance of one's life.

Some of you, for example, may have a statue of Quan Yin in your house. Do not make Quan Yin as something external to you. The statue comes from your own energy projection; you wish to form your own inner being as the beauty and perfection of Quan Yin. The statue itself is not important; it is what it represents. If you do form your inner being as beautiful and perfect, there is no difference between Buddhism and Taoism. You have already used the principle of Taoism in whatever you do. However, a person who worships Quan Yin as an external power as a source for becoming rich, strong or to get a beautiful lover is using it wrong. He does not know that he is going in the wrong direction and putting Quan Yin at an unreachable distance. All good things come from inside to outside, peacefully. It is not any attraction from outside that brings good things inside.

All good teachers have been good students. All good students who wish to be teachers or of real service to themselves need to have different practical experiences. If you do not experience different things, your experience and knowledge are limited. Then, whatever you do, your service to yourself is also limited.

There is confusion about the doctrine of emptiness that is taught in Buddhism and Taoism. When Buddhism teaches emptiness, it means the end of life is emptiness, and there is nothing worth living for. So there is emptiness. It is like a dream; the short life is over as quickly as lightning or dew on the leaves of an autumn day. But that teaching is different from the doctrine of emptiness in Taoism.

In the teaching of Tao, we use an empty mind. If your mind is empty, then you can accept something new into it. If your mind is full, then you cannot accept anything anymore. This expresses the function of empty mind which does not establish a conception of life. It means that an empty mind does not conceptualize life. Non-conceptualization is the Taoist purpose of practicing an empty mind. The empty mind can embrace the universe. The empty mind can help concentration and the empty mind helps the attainment of clarity. The empty mind can help people become objective. The empty mind can maintain itself as flexible. Also, one can also consider a positive use of the concept of emptiness: that conflicts themselves are empty and not worth fighting over. However, if a person generalizes the concept of emptiness to the point where he believes everything, including life, is empty, then he becomes incapable of rendering a positive contribution in his life.

You also know the fact that life is a continual situation. What you bring into this life determines if you will enjoy the next reincarnation. In reality, life is not really extinguishable. Once you deeply understand that, you will need a more advanced discussion. However, any conception can only be considered as an ideological tool. We have many tools; this is better than not having any. When people become stubborn and insist on using only a certain tool, the results are as inappropriate as using an axe to cut the vegetables for lunch. It is not the right tool. We need to learn to use the right tools. We take different ideas or conceptions as tools, learning how to utilize different ones to benefit our lives and the lives of those around us.

IV
Q: Would you talk about Zhan (Zen) Buddhism?

Master Ni: Zahn is originally from Chuang Tzu's teaching. It is Tao. When the new religion of Buddhism arrived from India and became popular, the Chinese spiritual people worked hard to reconcile it with Taoism. They fit the teaching of Tao into it and so it was revised. The ordinary people, government and political leaders became fanatic about it, wishing to become a superbeing like Buddha, without exercising the discipline to be so. That type of fanatic faith or belief is psychological deception. That group of spiritual leaders skillfully utilized Chuang Tzu's method to make Buddhism a new metaphor to teach the old truth of Tao, which is beyond all stories. They did an excellent job.

Unfortunately, the later followers of Zahn (Zen) were confused. They do not see that the true origin of Zen is a revelation or revolution; it is not a continuation of ordinary people's superstition or fanaticism. It is not fanaticism; it is truthful achievement. Buddha does not talk about any person being something else beyond his true spiritual nature. One only needs to be truthful, to be true to one's spiritual nature within.

First a person needs to discover his own spirituality. It is not an external search. Humans have their own spiritual nature, they awaken their own spiritual nature within. That spiritual nature is divinity within. They do not see the divine nature within, so they search for it externally by worshipping or establishing something fanatical. That attempt only comes back to suppress their true nature.

V

Q: My question is about chi. In Tai Chi Ch'uan classes, when your mind is there, the energy or chi will reach there. What is your personal experience? Please tell us.

Master Ni: I like to talk of the deeper sphere. It is chi. It is energy. The mind is energy. The formation of mentality is a formation of mind. Allow me to develop this. You see, in other religions, leaders put their conceptual creations above people's heads. They require that people worship and respect it, but not judge it. But in the practice of Tao, no conceptual creations are put above you. They are put beneath you. It can be judged or criticized. It can be used differently or explained differently, because it is conception. We are not going to fossilize your mind; you need to retain flexibility of mind.

Any conceptual creation or thought is a formation of your internal energy. How you think, react or view a thing is a formation of your internal energy. Some people will form a conception in a more extreme way and some people view a thing in a more gentle way. This is how the formation of internal energy differs from person to person. When you formalize your mind, your ideas will be different too. Your social and life background, physical condition, gender, age, education and cultural environment always underlie the limitations of your conceptual creation.

Today's problem of disharmony, on a worldly scale of nations or on a smaller scale of society and family, does not come from the reality of the situation. The real difficulty comes from the different conceptions, each one insisting on its own different conceptualized things. For example, a person stands in the foothills of a great mountain. The vista of this person must be different than the other people on different points of the mountain. People are not reasonable enough to understand that their conception comes from where they stand. Instead they fight over the differences.

This example of the mountain is similar to the story about the four blind men who have never seen an elephant, so each one feels it to find out what it is. One touches the trunk, one touches the ear, one touches the leg and one touches the tail. Each has his own impression of what an elephant is. When they discuss it, they end up fighting over whose description is right.

Today, there are many people who are mentally blind, and they fight. This is why the first teaching of Tao is to deconceptualize yourself. This is hard work for us. We would like to see harmony among all human people, all societies, families and friends. But the conceptual creations cause a big problem in today's world.

Q: Lao Tzu says to concentrate your energy and soften yourself to be like the life situation of a baby.

Master Ni: Most Taoist work is to teach students to deconceptualize the contamination accumulated from their life. A hard life makes people hardened or hard. An easy life makes people take life too lightly, giving rise to negligence which brings future trouble or mistakes. To be a student of Tao, the first thing is to deconceptualize yourself, but not only as it relates to the past. You need to do it every moment, because each moment is a fresh moment, a new situation. Do not bring a preconception into any new situation. Otherwise you mistreat others or mistreat yourself, or misjudge others or misjudge yourself. To have no preconception means to refresh your mind or maintain a fresh mind all the time.

Now we can talk about being a baby. Does a baby have a preconception in its mind? This is a metaphor for maintaining our minds and energy as a newborn baby does.

I can answer your question two ways. One way is a prevalent idea. When your life is like a baby, you give yourself so much potential for further development. If you are already formed for something, then you lose the flexibility. You cannot build anything or bring anything much better into your life. Only when you are very open, like a young, new life, can you give yourself better life opportunities and new chances. Otherwise, you treat yourself as a dead person, with things of the past.

This ability to keep an open mind is also associated with the skill of rejuvenation. When you do the practice of Tai Chi Ch'uan with discipline, it can make the contribution of regeneration for you. At the very least, it will slow down the aging process. So to become a baby is a high goal; we utilize all possible practices to reach the goal. It is positive. The Chinese medicinal herbs and the practice of golden immortal medicine, although it cannot bring you back as a dependent baby, can make your life condition so healthy and independent that in some ways it is a new life.

When a person performs Tai Chi Ch'uan, sometimes his palm feels warm or his fingers tingle. This is the energy flow coming into your palm. An achieved tai chi teacher can pick up and throw a much bigger or larger person ten yards, but that is not something that I like to promote.

You might like me to talk more about my personal experience. People like to borrow my personal experience to use as a mirror to see if anything from it can be of help to them. I think that in cultivating chi, the most important things is not to let any mental pressure or burden press us down. A person who takes too much mental pressure is like a flower that cannot blossom because of polluted air, deep snow, extreme temperature and so on. To nurture chi is to pacify and lessen the burden of one's mind. Calming the mind is the fundamental element or foundation of cultivation. When this has been accomplished, then we continue to work on the other requirements. If we are pressed down or poorly affected by our living, social or working environment, it is called "being robbed by one's external environment." If we experience pressure from internal impulses such as strong desires, we lose our calmness and peace and cannot harmonize with the natural energy in our environment. This is called "being robbed by one's internal environment." Both are incorrect ways of living and need to be corrected.

I know that each of you has a different life situation. No life situation is without trouble, problems or difficulties. But the outcome of your problems depends on how you view them and how you manage them. Some of you need so much time and energy to tackle your problems, that you do not have time to cultivate your energy.

To "cultivate Tao" is to cultivate our life being, our energy, our life energy. If, for example, your internal desire is too strong, you will not notice the potential outside obstruction, limitation or regulation; then what you do invites or causes trouble for yourself. By causing or reflecting the trouble back to yourself, you do not have a peaceful mind. If your mind is not relaxed, then you do not feel free to do what you wanted to do, and your life energy is in poor condition. It is not in normal growth.

So it is important for all of us to arrange or manage our psychological environment and psychological condition. If you do not do that well, then your practice will become mechanical and it will not be beneficial, true energy that will grow from your cultivation. If a person wishes to arrange a suitable psychological environment for energy cultivation, it is helpful to study Lao Tzu and Chuang Tzu. Chinese Buddhism is popular, but they use different terms. Practically, it has already been reformed by using Chinese language and receiving the influence of the teachings of Lao Tzu and Chuang Tzu when it was first translated into Chinese.

To the achieved Taoists, the whole teaching of Buddhism is a new metaphor that further develops the metaphoric teaching of Chuang Tzu. All those stories help

make one's psychological environment suitable for cultivating life energy. If you understand this, and you have a
positive attitude, then all the existing or developing teaching in China or abroad can help you without discrimination
of religious membership.

One can utilize existing spiritual teaching and spiritual
education to protect oneself and to cultivate and nurse
one's life energy. We need to make an adjustment to protect the sprout and blossom of our personal spiritual development in our own garden. Experienced teachers help by
passing down their teachings to clarify our psychological
confusion and trouble.

All of us are now in a new environment. This new
environment is short in history; thus it also has less of a
historical burden. We need to utilize this new environment
to cultivate our energy. But do not make trouble for yourself by putting your nose in everything. If a person's mind
is too active or if he has many unnatural desires, then he
cannot cultivate his energy at all because he is being
pushed towards all kinds of activity to attain worldly interests. Then how does he expect to nurse his internal baby?
Then how can he conceive the holy fetus within? It is impossible. So first of all, we learn from the sages to regulate
our life and mind, eliminate all unnecessary activities and
only do that which correctly maintains our good life and
well being. Then, a person will notice that he is doing better, too.

During Tai Chi Ch'uan practice, it is not helpful to
think about combat or fighting with somebody. Just do it
as a pure energy exercise. This peace will become supportive in nurturing your energy. If you have any other
thoughts during your Tai Chi practice, then your Tai Chi
practice is not helpful. Once you are doing all right, the
energy itself will grow naturally. Like our ancestors, you
will feel as though you are bathing in a warm spring breeze.
You feel so good because your energy is producing, affecting. This kind of nice feeling is a result or an experience of
one's own cultivation. It is not artificial, something caused
by taking a drug like LSD to make you feel good. Drugs do
harm to a person. But Tai Chi Ch'uan is a true way to

nurture your true energy. When the chi comes to a certain part of the body, you feel it. For example, if you bring the chi to your head, you might feel as though you have a thousand ants scratching or that you have some itching on the skin of the head. It is not a bad feeling; it is a very pleasant feeling, difficult to describe. This kind of happiness, joy and pleasant feeling is the high condition of the harmony of the union of your life being, and all elements now put together produce the best energy for you.

Remember one important thing: in cultivating yourself, the best cultivation is your daily life. So keep your peaceful, regulated life schedule, with daily constancy. Keep it steady, keep it constant. In that way, you do not need to use your mind to think about each day arranging your life differently. You have time to let your energy grow naturally in the consistency of your lifestyle.

About 50 years ago, there was a man named Master Li Ching Yun, who was 250 years old. This man lived a simple life in a village which is how he could live so long. When he was young, Master Li gathered and sold herbs to make a living. When he became old, almost the whole village were his descendants. Unfortunately, during his lifetime there was a warlord named Yang Sen, who was a general. Yang Sen was curious about all the strange things he had heard about, including the art of longevity. He invited the 250-year-old master to come to the capital. The old man was accustomed to living on simple food, but in the capital he was served the tasty Chinese dishes like those from a Chinese restaurant. Suddenly, because of the change in his life by coming to the city, receiving the respect of many people and eating different food, he died.

This true story tells you that an ordinary, simple life is more supportive than exciting occasions of having a good time. That good time is not more supportive than a simple life. To live a long and healthy life, it is not helpful to admire big banquets. Do not admire the fun and pleasure of joining a big group in a party, but remain simple and have a humble life. That is the most supportive element in cultivating Tao.

Make your simple life centered, yet allow yourself to be open enough to make a positive contribution in any possible opportunity. For example, now you are organized in a Tai Chi club. Some of you are leaders and others offer their time to do this or that. This is all constructive contribution. Any constructive contribution will come back to you. It will make your energy higher than if you just remain yourself. Conversely, a person can darken his energy by misbehavior, so we never allow ourselves to think badly, talk badly or do badly. Whatever you do, you are the one who lightens or darkens your life energy. When your energy is light, then your energy will ascend. When your energy is heavy, and too associated with the material world, your energy will descend.

This is how the many ancestors who cultivated chi ascended to the high sphere of the spiritual world. In the Tang dynasty, there was a great scholar called Hangyu. He did not put much trust in any religious teaching. At that time, there was also a young girl in Szechuan province whose name was Shi Tzu An. She was pure; she started her cultivation when she was nine years old. When she was a teenager, she was able to fly in the daytime. Many people witnessed that feat, and the scholar Hangyu wrote a poem about her to make a record in Chinese literature.

If we wish to cultivate our energy, to cultivate the Tao, we must have objective, scientific attitudes. We cannot be superstitious. We are looking for fact. If we become superstitious, we fall into the trap of the devil. The devil will hold your nose and bring you to further darkness. The true way of cultivation is the Tao. Any religious emphasis is the sacrifice of one's self to attain a conceptual result. That is the most evil thing a person could experience in spiritual cultivation. So a person who wishes to nurture chi or to attain Tao first needs to understand and attain enough knowledge to not be misguided by anyone.

In your cultivation, the most important thing is to maintain clarity in your mind. If you lose the clarity of your mind, you only see many beautiful visions. They are not true. They are the devil's traps; practically, they are your own mixed spiritual images. If you maintain your spiritual nature in clarity, there is God. There is a governed world. There is order in the universe. This cannot be neglected. It is not necessary to be a follower of a certain religion, but each one of us must have a spiritual cultivation, a spiritual life. A spiritual life is much broader than the limitation of a religion. Though all of you can utilize the general reading material of religion or general study of religion as the support of your spiritual life, do not be limited or confined by certain conceptions, nor utilize only one metaphoric system and decide it is truth. Once you respect your own spirit, you can objectively utilize all different teachings to assist your clarity. Cultivation is not to make yourself live in the dark by any narrow religious construction. If the different ways of speaking, different explanations and different expressions do not confuse you, they are all metaphors to tell you something indescribable. Read between the lines and above the lines to understand the true form and true spiritual reality. That is a true achievement; otherwise, a person is bound tightly by a rope made of words from someone else's mouth and saliva.

Chi is more profound than the ordinary physical force produced by muscle. That is easily understood. When I was young, I was also interested in the popular martial arts, because with only one punch, you can immediately see the result. But Tai Chi Ch'uan is different. After I had a chance to experience the profundity, the achievement, the principle of the softness that can overcome the hardness which can be proven in physical combat, then slowly it made me more interested in looking for the cultivation of chi. Generally, physical force is easily understood, but chi is much harder to understand. I remember that after decades of intense practice of Tai Chi Ch'uan, I understood that it is a slow movement. It is not a physical movement, it is an internal chi movement.

Once I experienced walking on the side of the street and being aware that somebody was doing and practicing chi exercise, although I could not see him. This was because the range of one's energy or chi is much wider than that of physical energy. Usually if somebody practices ordinary martial arts or fights in the neighborhood, if they do not make any noise, you do not even know that they are there. The person is so quiet in movement, thus he attains the internal flow of chi. Chi is responsive. Far away, it is not reached by eyesight or by the scope of one's hearing capability; nor is it something a person can touch. It is nothing that can be seen, but you can feel it.

Any place I have been where they have learned or taught Tai Chi Ch'uan, it is much easier for the people to know who I am. Our communication and affinity is easy because the internal chi response is harmonized; the same pattern of chi works. That comes close to reaching a spiritual level. It depends on one's personal practice, because people's energy formation is different. A person who does well in Tai Chi Ch'uan not only has a face that looks different, but his words, movements, actions and everything are different because he has cultivated that harmonious chi within him. His life being presents the harmonious chi.

All people grow from the external, shallow sphere to the deep sphere and from external truth to the deep internal truth. I believe that the experience I had as a youth learning martial arts is a common experience for many people. When young, people do not know too much, only a little bit. When one's understanding grows, I believe that it is a truthful, precious thing that can be reached. In the mainland and outside, I met many masters who were really doing well in their Tai Chi Ch'uan arts. They are like gentlemen; they are not forceful at all, but once they engage in play with a strong muscular person, they can manage him as easily as an adult manages a child. It comes from their true achievement, but they are usually never aggressive. They are so gentle. They can truly present the culture of ancient China. Also, they can present the true culture, true spirit and species of a human being.

Your question is how to gather one's ching, chi and shen, which means sexual energy, physical force, emotional force and spiritual power together in one, as the principle of Taoist cultivation. But first you need to understand that the physical refined energy in a different level is much more subtle than what is seeable, audible, reachable and touchable. From this level, you can go even higher. Otherwise, you only become amazed and feel strange, and can never really enter the sphere of reality, the inner room of truthful practice.

There are two ways to help nurture chi. The main practice is being quiet or in meditation; that is sitting quietly and using a breathing practice that helps you nurture chi. Do this each day and night. Traditionally, the day was divided into four quarters: 12:00 midnight, 6:00 a.m., 12:00 noon, and 6:00 p.m. The Taoist adepts practiced meditation at those times. A person's practice is different at different times of the day.

You have touched upon one of the Taoist practices, Tai Chi Ch'uan, which the students have performed today. Of the many ways to nurture chi such as meditation and breathing, Tai Chi Ch'uan is also an important practice. Tai Chi Ch'uan is a beneficial system of chi gong which organizes quietude and stillness of movement. When in movement there is stillness, when in stillness there is movement; both can help one generate energy. The first step to learning how to nurture chi is to understand chi. If you understand it and have a little experience, then it will bring confidence to you. You can even be helped by seeing someone's good example. Then you can continue from this beginning to go further.

When you do Tai Chi Ch'uan with concentration, by centering your own life, your energy naturally generates and grows. This is not easily seen, but doing it day by day, your health and physical condition will be greatly improved and the endurance of life can be attained. Using no physical force, by achievement you learn and reach the level of chi. From the achievement of chi, you can go to reach the subtle level of shen or spirit. It would be too difficult for a person to jump directly to the spiritual level.

In a typical society, people usually have one of two kinds of attitudes about spiritual energy. If they hold an intellectual attitude, they do not believe it, because they have not had a chance to experience it. The other type of attitude is a conventional, following type of attitude characterized by religious believers. Similarly, these people do not have a chance to experience spiritual energy, they just trust and follow what somebody else has said. In either case, the result is not accurate. I call our way "self-cultivation" because you need self; you need your own life being to extend to a different level, then you come to a different level of being.

At present, in mainland China, no religion really exists. Religions are for tourist business. But they need chi gong to help the health of the general population, so chi gong is still popular. Even though their dogma does not agree that there is spirit, if there is development of chi gong, they must go further, deeper, until they reach the spiritual level. When people discover that there is nothing else - spirit - it will bring them to the verge of collapse of materialism, which is the rigid philosophical foundation of Communism. In the reality of the universe, spiritual energy is not materialism. Neither is it idealism or religious beliefs. It is the universal natural vitality.

Fighting is negative, useless and meaningless. As students of chi, we need practical, matter of fact attitudes, step-by-step scientific attitudes. We need to look for full achievement without fooling ourselves by listening to someone else's description or to someone with a negative attitude toward the existence of the high level of life energy.

Today's learning environment for modern people is different from that of the ancient people. Ancient people learned from what the teacher said. They did not have any difficulty or obstacle in accepting the teachings, so their achievement was much faster. Today, because we are intellectually educated, we have a lot of trouble believing in the existence of spiritual energy. However, the benefit of our intellectual education is that we are more objective.

Dear friends, I talk about all possible achievements and the different truthful levels of life energy. Let me be serious and recommend that all of you keep yourself in the chi level without going up too high to the delicate spiritual level. The reason is that if your energy becomes too subtle, modern life with its noise, speed and unnatural creations might conflict with your development. You become so subtle that if a thousand miles or a million light years away something happens, it is as if it happens in your own back yard. You know everything. Then how will you stand the noise? Even the airplanes in the sky shake the air, at the same time vibrating your physical life being. If you become very delicate, subtle and gentle, you feel that.

It is nice for a person to have the ambition to achieve immortal life. However, as long as a person still has a body, he is still more or less affected by physical law, so there will be some discomfort in spiritual cultivation, such as when one is disturbed by the noise from machines. The natural world has no mechanical development, and because the scope of one's spiritual power is so wide, a person can enjoy reaching everywhere. Truthfully, the size of a person's life being is not determined by the size of the physical being; it is much bigger. For example, as you sit here, an airplane has flown into your lung. You do not believe me when I tell you of your great size, but your true being is much bigger than the physical reality of who you are. If more people would develop themselves spiritually, fewer disturbances would be created: people would all want fewer noisy machines and less pollution in the world.

Doing something to improve your health is most important. You do not need special training or a special teacher to teach you anything higher than that. Although people are equipped with three spheres of energy, with only partial development they shall have difficulty. A person who becomes more spiritual, more delicate and sensitive will have more difficulty in the modern world as conditions worsen.

The traditional books of Tao are mostly collected in the *Taoist Canon*. The vast *Taoist Canon* takes a long time to study and read. Most of its contents are junk. Only the ones already developed, who have had special instruction, or have a special eye and can see the true blue sky above the clouds, can understand it. Any undeveloped person in the general public will not see any value in the true teachings and therefore will not respect them. Even if a person is interested in the *Canon* and reads or ask someone to translate it for him, he will still not understand it without special training.

All of you know about the problem of the Chinese Communists, Mao Tse Tung and the so-called ten-year cultural

revolution. Why did such a violent episode of history occur? It happened because the perpetrators did not understand the achievement of the ancient developed ones.
There is a gap which cut off the ancient achievement from
the later developed mind. What the later people do not
understand, they do not believe or trust. So they destroy it
from their lack of respect for high achievement and reality.
Now, because there are not enough doctors or hospitals to
take care of patients, they are helpless to stop the study of
chi gong, so they let Chi Gong continue and develop.
Things such as Chi Gong offer great proof of the advantage
of ancient culture and development.

If one were to make a comparison between ancient and
modern times, one would find that there were many highly
developed persons in ancient China. Such individuals were
more developed than the society they lived in. If we compare the societies and modern nations of the west with
modern China, we will see that China is undeveloped, not
only in technology but also politics. This is because in the
past 2,500 years, her leaders still hold thoughts of evil
monarchy rather than of a healthy, serving monarchy of the
times before.

Let us talk about the later monarchies, kings and emperors. Those rulers enjoyed tremendous wealth, more
than everybody else. Also they had the desire to live forever, so they allowed Chi Gong to develop without suppressing it. Now, Chi Gong is the only hope, the only light,
the only achievement we have still remaining in China of
spiritual culture. Anything that was against the desire of
the monarch was destroyed. Did those emperors or kings
live long? No, they did not. Why? Because spiritual
achievement is not only physical, it requires spiritual development; bloody hands can never live long. That is heavenly
law.

We can observe and compare to see who was achieved
according to the standard of physical longevity. Many people who live in mountains or a rural place live to be very
old. But people who tremendously enjoy the physical
sphere of the senses are usually short lived; so most monarchs die young, not even living as old as normal people,

because they have death on their own bloody hands or on the bloody hands of their ancestors who created monarchy.

The secret of life is that once your material sphere is strong enough to support your life, you have an opportunity to gather your mind, spirit and physical energy to engage in the enterprise of a long, healthy life. But how can people with unlimited material desire live long? Once they are more materially expanded, then those people's spiritual development diminishes. It is necessary that they die early because they have lost their balance.

Tao is most public; it belongs to anyone. There is no secret in Taoist teaching; but its profundity truly impresses people, so they think it is secret and mysterious. Many teachers are selfish and do not give the true teaching or method to ordinary students. This is because either the teacher is not highly achieved, or the student has not yet come to the right stage and the teacher has difficulty talking about it with the student. Although T'ai Chi Ch'uan is only one achievement as a tool, some teachers do not like to tell the truth of how to achieve excellence because some side practices involve their professional secret. So they teach a method just for people to attain regular health.

Some people are looking for high achievement to become a champion; however, truthfully speaking, regular health is more important and more valuable. The fierce martial art that makes people champions is also the art that makes people short lived. They think they have easily learned a simple thing; they do not know what they have learned. The simple Tai Chi movement is more real and contributive to learning than the secret side practices.

Ambitiously, most young people also wish to learn the teachers' secrets of how to become a champion in fighting, but those teachers wish to protect their personal prestige and reputation. They do not easily let the knowledge of how they were trained and became achieved became known to the students. Such teachers are proud of their skill in pushing hands, but it is a side dish, not the main meal. If I am allowed to say it, martial arts, if done only on that level, have no truly high value in spirit.

Therefore, my recommendation for all of you is not to look for the secret of how to become a champion in martial arts. In the sphere of Tai Chi, what the teachers promote for health is still the best offering.

The ancient books are the most trustworthy for today. Today you can make a living by writing, so people become very active and productive by writing. In ancient times, people would rather spend time discovering and knowing something useful for themselves rather than writing to make extra money. So the ancient books are simple, but they contain essence. The setback is that sometimes they are difficult to understand without a suitable explanation or side explanation. I feel I am obliged to explain it, because I was so educated when I was young, and it took much time to learn the ancient achievement. So whatever I produce, I still present the ancient achievement in modern language.

Thirteen years ago, when I was in Taiwan, I wrote several important Taoist books and some books on Chinese medicine in Chinese. Some of my books specialize on Tai Chi Ch'uan. When I wrote the books, it was with serious spirit. I really wished to pass the precious treasures to other people without their being kept by me. Among my students, I also gave some more profound teachings. In Taiwan, they have organized the Union of Heaven and People and in Tai Chung, the Association of the Union of Heaven and People.

The old written Chinese language is difficult for the new descendants of the recent generations. So after I came to the United States, I took advantage of the communicative English, and have written all my books with the communication trait of English. This was so all the profound teachings of ancient achievement could be easily understood by all people. Sometimes people say to me, jestingly, that if people in the future wish to learn Taoism, they need first to learn English, then read my books!

In Taoism, we worship the three types of purity. They are called the three ching; ching means cleanness and purity. When a person's body is pure, it means he does not have any sickness. When his mind is clean and pure, he does not have any troubles or worries. When his spirit is clean and pure, he remains in clarity and is not confused nor loses his vision. That is what we worship. So the true student of Tao learns something for himself. He works on himself because the sang ching, three purities, are within himself. This is not going to a temple to worship the ones cut in wood. Yes, the wooden figures can also be a spiritual symbol. But the main thing is: you need to work with yourself.

There was a great master called Yung Mung, the Gate of Clouds. Once he was talking about Buddha with a group of people. The people asked him, "What is Buddha?" Now, can you tell me what Yung Mung said?

Someone in Audience: Gang shi chuech.

Someone else in Audience: What is gang shi chuech?

Master Ni: (Hesitates) I do not know if I should say it. If a person walks by the roadside, they see that sometimes dogs and cats leave their messes there. The dry stuff on the roadside is gang shi chuech. It means that people do not value their own essence but value things like dry feces at the roadside. It directly tells that most people use their alive spirit to worship the unworthy dead statues; that is what happens to the worshippers of Buddha statues. This is what happens to all religious believers. They do not know the truly alive divinity within. This is how the true master told them directly about it.

I prefer to use a different metaphor if I am allowed. But so far, even a highly educated gentleman finds it hard to understand what the master says about it.

I think everyone has heard the story about when Sakyamuni was born. In case you have not, I will repeat it. There is a story that seven days after Sakyamuni was born, the baby stood up and walked on the ground with one hand pointed towards heaven and the other hand pointed towards the ground. He declared, "Above high heaven, beneath low earth, I am the most venerable." What was the meaning of that?

Someone in the Audience: Yung Mung said, "If I saw such a baby, I would use a stick to beat it to death and let a dog eat it. It is not a human being, it is a monster."

Master Ni: You must understand, Yang Mung was not as crude as that. He meant the baby, or the belief in that story, is not truthful; it is the fanatic mind of people and the storyteller who used it. Nobody in seven days stands up to walk or talk with language like that. That is an dishonest way of religious promotion. Yung Mung was the one who so courageously pointed it out, but the emperors and common people worshipped it as truth. The common people still worship those beliefs, even to this day.

How could Yang Mung have the courage to say such things? He was not afraid of any external divinity or that some god might punish him. Why did he have this courage and you do not? Because he saw the truth; he had reached the truth. So the descendants, the ordinary Chinese people, have all declined, fallen down without that spiritual achievement that enables them to see the truth. Such a clear spirit of truth lives within ourself, but people themselves cannot see it. People throw that genuine spiritual truth away and replace it with pebbles and sawdust of external learning.

The modern Chinese only know to worship external establishments without worshipping the spiritual truth or divine nature within. This is how communism can develop as a religion. Now Chinese society has fallen into the trap of a new ideology of Communism. What can this new ideology bring to people? It is a new superstition, a new psychological trap, the same as in the past. The majority of people have lost their clarity. It is a continuation of monarchy in a different shape: that of a few gangsters. The natural society of the entire country of China has come to its darkest hours. All Chinese people of intellectual development of natural inspiration can find the true light instead of using artificial conceptual creation as an excuse for personal or national failure.

Q: In the history books it is written that Zhan (Zen) Buddhism was developed by Bodhidharma, an Indian teacher who came to China to inspire the Chinese people.

Master Ni: With the same truthful attitude with which Master Yung Mung taught people, and with my fresh mind of youth, when I studied the tai ching of Hui Neng, the Sixth Patriarch of the Zahn (Zen) tradition, I discovered that his teaching is totally unified with the teaching of Tao. But I wondered how that could be, because his teaching became Buddhism. In the Zahn books, it is clearly referred that Zahn (Zen) was started by Bodhidharma.

When the Sixth Patriarch came from the north back to the south, for 15 years he lived with hunters. When he chose a place to start his teaching, he selected a piece of new land, north of Canton, in the mountains which are in the southern part of China.

The center of Chinese society at that time was in the north, then it gradually developed south. So during his time, the south was not yet developed. When the people of the political center did not like someone, they exiled them to the undeveloped south. The land and waterways had no names, and so the names of the places were chosen by the individuals who settled there. Hui Neng called the stream in the new location as Tsao stream, and called his small hut, which later became a temple, as Nang Hua temple. Why was that stream called Tsao? Why was the temple called Nang Hua? The names Hui Neng selected clearly imply the true origin of his teaching. He picked them because Chuang Tzu was born in Nang Hua village, of Tsao county in the province of San Tung. Chuang Tzu's book, with the respectable title *Nang Hua Ching*, which means the Script of the Flower of the Warm South, ranks next to Lao Tzu's *Tao Teh Ching* in importance of other Taoist books. Ching means ancient instruction or guidance. Zahn (Zen) Buddhism was not widely recognized; it was unknown and did not become popular until the teaching of the sixth patriarch.

The teaching of Zahn (Zen) Buddhism is different from Buddhism. In Buddhism, Buddha is worshipped and the desired result of this worship is to become a super being or Buddha and enjoy being a super spiritual authority. But Master Hui Neng, the sixth patriarch instructed, "In my teaching, I do not say to worship Buddha to become Buddha. My teaching is only to concentrate on ming sing jen sing, which means to know your spiritual nature and return to the divinity within." His teaching totally changed the external worship of Buddhism.

In the teaching of Buddhism, there are so many scriptures. Because those translations have an Indian word here and there, people do not clearly see the meaning, which produces a mysterious feeling. That became a big attraction to some scholars and the masses of people. However, starting with Hui Neng, it has been denied that there is any importance to the written script, because it is one's own spiritual nature that is most venerable, respectable and more important than any external description.

Recently I produced a book called *Enlightenment: Mother of Spiritual Independence* and two other books, called *The Way of Integral Life* and *Attaining Unlimited Life*. That set of books really touches this misguidance with the intent to correct people's misconceptions.

Buddhism has been active in China for more than 1,000 years. Because some Zen Master did not straightly declare his background, he played with most people's faith to enlighten the common believers. Some became achieved, but some stayed on the religious path. However, in either case, nobody really clearly saw the relationship between Zahn Buddhism and Buddhism; this even caused confusion in the Chinese culture, like the new Confucianism that developed during the Sung Dynasty. They dare not openly accept Zahn Buddhism which contains the teaching of Tao. These scholars were unable to see Zahn as a new reflection of the ancient enlightened mind of Tao.

Sakyamuni was a great teacher. He is not the one who should take any blame or responsibility for any later development. In India during his time, the worship of all kinds of natural spirits and ghosts was quite popular. He was the first one who directly promoted the understanding of life as a new spiritual attitude. But unfortunately, 500 years after he passed away, his philosophy was not widely respected or studied. Some new leaders combined Buddha's teaching with Hinduism, but still used the psychology of general society which worships Buddha as a super-being. New leaders used all kinds of earlier Indian superficial beliefs to develop a new Buddhism.

Then we come to Hui Neng, a great teacher with the power to tell the truth. Except for him, all the students of later generations who studied Buddhism lost the spirit of the original teacher; they could not find the true gold of spirit within themselves any more. They only engaged in eating saliva; by this I mean, they only take the words from other people without engaging in truthful searching, discovery and restoration of their own natural spirit.

However, the highest achievement of Buddha's teaching is to look for so-called nirvana, peaceful mind, because of the trouble-mindedness of everyday life. Sakyamuni gave up the style of everyday life to live in the trees with a simple life of a beggar. Each day, one meal sustained his life for him to engage in his spiritual search. This allowed him to maintain his peace of mind within without being torn by any worldly obligations. From this point, you learn that his initial motivation is different from the motivation of the ancestors of the Chinese region.

You know, the Chinese have their Chinese spiritual tradition and the Indians have their Indian spiritual tradition. When two pieces of stone touch each other, a beautiful spark is produced. This is to say that any internal development needs or comes from external stimulation. Without external stimulation, personal development will become dried up. If it does not turn out to be self-pride, one's achievement will become stiffened. So all new development or improvement has come through a situation of trouble. It can be a correct response to a challenge by adopting a new positive inspiration to reform the old life. To make a new development or improvement, some people are inspired and spiritually reincarnate so they can come to make the correct response to the challenge.

The Zahn (Zen) masters were most active in the Tang Dynasty; now let us go further down to the Sung Dynasty.[3] At that time, a great Taoist teacher named Chen Tuan[4] brought back the teaching of the *I Ching* to the public and to the field of scholars. This allowed the scholars to recognize and reevaluate the truthful, unbreakable teaching experience of the *I Ching*. From Chen Tuan, a new cultural trend developed, which in China was called the study of spiritual law, li (law) or Tao. Although Chen Tuan brought a new cultural trend, many of the later great teachers of the Sung Dynasty of this new school still did not know the real origin of Zahn (Zen) Buddhism, which is Tao. In other words, although they began to unify their new teaching with Zahn and Tao, they did not know that the origin was the same. Many people who came after the scholars and gave new commentaries still think Zahn is Buddhism, but that is because they do not see its true origin.

I would like to talk about Bodhidharma. As you know, he is a faithful-looking person with a big nose, beard and moustache, and a strong body. He was a writer of Indian spiritual work. He produced one or two booklets that were translated into Chinese. The person was never in China; even if he had been in China, he produced no influence there. The forerunners of Zen employed his name because his background was not clearly written anywhere. He was chosen as the image for leadership in association with Buddhism to accomplish its main goal of enlightening the believers.

You have heard the story that the dharma came to China by riding a piece of reed branch. In ancient times, the painters' brush was made of reed, so the image refers to the calligrapher's pen rather than a literal person riding on a reed branch. At that time, Chinese culture had been long lost; the dying ash needed a new stir. The majority needed

---

[3]960-1279 A.D.

[4]Around 988 A.D.

a new spiritual image. That group of profound scholars needed to find a way to educate the majority, and that was how they did it. The forerunners of Zahn, the scholars, thought it was a challenge of the time, but they truly faithfully used the method Chuang Tzu had developed. That is to use metaphors to teach the truth. They discovered that was a good way to do it, then they realized that they had succeeded. So Zen Buddhism became exceptionally popular, not only in China but also in Japan and Korea.

Unfortunately, now in our time, the true spirit and achievement of Zen Buddhism has also died. All that is left is a group of people attached to the dead shell from which the meat has gone.

Awakening has no boundary. It is not only for people in the west or east or in the north or south; there is no limit to the number of people in any certain region that can awaken. Master Liu Shen Shang, a master of the later school of new Taoism, said, "Whenever a sage is born, (for example the sage of the west,) if he reaches the truth, it must be the same truth as that reached by the sage of the east." It means that not only can an Indian attain enlightenment; but anyone can.

So the group of Zen masters was really awakened by the decline of their society's spirit. Their motivation was truly not to fool people; they needed to adapt to the psychological spiritual situation of development of their time. That was what was needed, and that was how it was done.

There is a parable that says when Seng Guan, the second master of Zen, extended his hope to learn from Bodhidharma, Bodhidharma said to him, "First cut off your arm, then I will teach you." Now, everybody thought that this story was true, that the person actually cut off his arm to look for the precious teaching of enlightenment. But it was not true; it was just a metaphor to describe how valuable the truth is.

Let me tell you this. Someone in this group asked me how we gather, converge and unify the three spheres of energy inside the body. If you came to ask me to teach it to you, and I said, "Pay me," if it was important to you, you would pay me. If I said, "Cut off your arm before I will teach you," would you really go that far? Can such a story be accepted as truth? Do you accept it? However, it was a touching story.

People use a striking story to build a new faith, however, the masters, with bamboo whip in hand, demanded that the students sitting in front of them stay awake. They would beat them if they fell asleep. They would say, "if you wish to learn dharma, you have to wake up. Wake up!" But they did not wake up as the Master meant. He meant to wake up their minds, not just their bodies. You see, people are always confused by stories; they mistake them for a true history instead of a metaphor. Thus, the stories keep them asleep. The masters try to teach enlightenment, not a literal story. This is the trouble which confuses the mind. The confused head should receive the beating of the teacher, so awakening might happen.

Teachers depend on the structure of telling those stories to maintain people's attraction to truly teach something to them. How the stories are understood is not the stage of the instructors; it is people's stage of ungrowth. One of the great masters once said: "Everybody come to worship Buddha, but any time I say the word Buddha, I need to wash my mouth three times in order to clean it after that."

Q: I believe that Indian Buddhism also received the influence from the north, which is the teaching of the I Ching.

Master Ni: We cannot assertively say that Indian Buddhism originated from the *I Ching*. However, the main structure of Buddhist philosophy describes the world as having four stages. The first stage is accomplishing, the second stage is to keep what is accomplished, the third stage is destruction and the fourth stage becomes empty to conclude all lives. I do not think it is beyond the vision of the *I Ching* and to see the changes.

Q: So finally the world becomes empty, or any establishment becomes empty again. To me, it sounds like Lao Tzu in the Tao Teh Ching. The first two lines say, "Tao cou tao, ti tsan tao; min cou ming, li tsan ming" or "Tao, as the absolute way of the universe, cannot be conveyed with words." That means it is indescribable, but everything becomes the same, indescribable and undefinable; the reality of the world exists like that.

Master Ni: There is the unspeakable, indescribable truth as Tao.   Also, there is the speakable and the describable Tao. In its depth, it is unspeakable, but now, what we are talking about it, is speakable. We use the speakable sphere to reach the unspeakable sphere. This is our method, and it is what I am doing now.   The ι speakable Tao is your personal experience.   Even if you describe it, it sounds different from what it is.   So what is enlightenment?   One master once said, describing enlightenment is like an the situation of an enlightened person hanging from a cliff halfway in the sky.   Above him, there is nothing reachable to grab or grasp, below him there is nothing to catch him, and with his mouth he is biting a thin branch that is holding him on the cliff.   Now do you ask him what Tao is?   If he answers, he will fall down a thousand feet and become pieces.   So Tao is something that when you are enlightened, it is difficult to describe.

Enlightenment is like a person who is bathing or swimming in a river; whether it is warm or cold is totally known to him, but it is not known to the one standing on the shore.   What the enlightened ones achieve is unspeakable in that moment.   What we achieve is the speakable Tao; with this we wish to reach the unspeakable Tao.

The Zen master always asks a question. If the student tries to answer, he immediately beats him to stop him from talking.   But any answer is a guess. I think this, you think that, it is all a kind of theoretical development, a kind of play of mind or the performance of one's mentality.   It is not the stage of the action, the doing and the doer, being united all at the same time without any slight separation.

Tao is what is already there. You do not need to guess, you do not need to think.   If you are thinking, it is already second thoughts, it is not the reality of that moment.

I do not worry about your knowing the secret of Tao, the enlightenment of Zen.   It is not that you cannot understand. You can understand better. Your mind is always searching in flow. There is the unchangeable sphere and there is also a changeable sphere; you need to put forth your effort to unite them. Description is a different stage of spiritual condition: it is a splitting. It is not unification; it is not united.

Does the high truth need practice? For most people, yes. They need to break through the dust and clouds to see the truth. The one who lives in the light is light and needs no further searching. But most students cannot stay in the light often, they always come back to the darkness again. This is why many struggle and play yo yo, up and down, up and down, their whole life in this dilemma.

The philosophy of the four stages is accomplishing or establishing, staying there, declining and then becoming empty. However, the philosophy of Taoism does not leave a person with destruction or emptiness. Such a philosophy would induce a pessimistic attitude toward life. There is always the hope of coming back again.

The *I Ching* has the correct understanding. The *I Ching* does not mind destruction or a bad time. Bad times or destruction always sows new seeds. The *I Ching* brings about new confidence and new hope as a truthful, natural cycle. The *I Ching* gives the whole universal truth, not just part. Most people are dismayed by the whole truth of life, which includes the fact that destruction is not malevolent.

The population of human society is growing, but the instinct of human people has not changed. Wars are the expression of the incorrectly conducted sexual energy of males. So there is war. All monarchs are established by war. Similarly, the male leader horse in a group of horses is the strongest one. None of this is based on spiritual achievement or development; so the worldly destructive cycle always appears again and again, until true spiritual development is attained by everyone.

The democratic system is a transformation of feminine energy. The negative expression of feminine energy is jealousy or speaking evil as attacking or criticizing behind somebody's back; it all points to fighting with words. Thus, competition for leadership in the democratic system is the same as women talking evil about each other. Mostly, no straightness or righteousness is seen.

What spiritual achievement has been reached in this century? Or any century? Not until people can achieve themselves to be above the low sphere dominated by physical energy can the true light of human development be seen. But we must also admit that even though democracy is a form of conflict in terms of two fellows arguing or competing, it generally results in stable, peaceful conditions for the people in the nation who nonetheless remain uninvolved in that competition for material supremacy!

Master Ni's Conclusion to this Discussion:

> *People wish to cultivate Tao*
> > *But Tao cannot be traced.*
> *People search for the ultimate truth.*
> > *But the ultimate truth cannot be acquired.*
> *The lost one cannot see the subtle law*
> > *behind the formed and the unformed.*
> *The one who has reached it,*
> > *knows that there is nothing that can be followed*
> > *and nothing that can be disobeyed.*
> > *as long as one does not go beyond one's nature.*
> *Among all good teachings,*
> > *the teaching of the most truthful essence*
> > *is not far away.*
> *Only by looking at your own place,*
> > *will you find it.*
> *There is no need to search far.*
> *It makes no use of wide scope of different knowledge.*
> *It gives no room for wit and eloquence.*
> *It has no connection with the months, long or short.*
> *It has no relationship with the ordinary year*
> > *or leap year.*

> *From trouble, wisdom arises.*
> *From dirt comes purity.*
> *People come to consult with me*
> > *about the high truth.*

I cannot make it be seen.
In the morning, I eat my breakfast.
At the next meal, I eat again.
Today, I am as natural as I am.
Tomorrow, I am the same.
Though there is clarity in my mind
However, I still appear to others as the foolish man.

(Note: The questions about Tai Chi Ch'uan which do not appear here will be published in Master Ni's forthcoming book about Tai Chi Ch'uan.)

TAOIST SPIRITUAL GROWTH

I
Necessity is the Mother of Invention

Q: I would like to ask about deepening one's spiritual cultivation: how can I reach God?

Master Ni: Seeing your great sincerity and purity impresses me with the image of a god before he reaches his development, as he questions himself. To answer your question, I also need to gather a similar pure energy to respond to your serious search.

We will go through the similar stages of ancient people's enlightenment. By studying this reality, we may guide ourselves to reach God. It seems that no simple answer can help you enter the depth or core of spirit. Delicacy of mind and patience with words are necessary to trace back to where and how people became lost or separated from universal spirituality. By their hectic life experience, most people have lost their connection with their own spiritual nature. This story cannot be shortened.

My teaching is the path of internal growth, which is derived from both external experience and the response to it. It is important for you to review the external aspects of unaffected, natural spiritual development as essential support for your proper future growth.

The original race of human people in China began at the headwaters of the Yellow River, in the province now called Chinghai, which borders the Middle Eastern countries where the Arabic races flourish.

In China, we believe the first human ancestor or the first known powerful person was Pang Gu. Pang Gu, as expressed by the legend, represents universal beingness. He is the entirety of nature; the entire universe is his being and we are just a part of his enormous being. This theory is a metaphor.

There is also some implication that Pang Gu was the first ruler when the human race was going through long periods of darkness or natural scatteredness and there was not yet any established human society or ruler.

Pang Gu was the first being; the supposition that he was the first ruler practically implies the conception of God.

All talk about Pang Gu is only a conjecture in response to the question the human race poses: "Where do we come from?" When I was a child, the serious answer to this question that my father, mother and elders gave me was that the first ancestor was Pang Gu. He lived far earlier than the development of written language; many uncountable years ago when no records were kept. However, nature is his being; thus, nature is his record. Written language has existed no more than 5,000 or 6,000 years. This is a very brief period when compared to the period of human existence before writing appeared and historical documents were kept.

Written history is also interesting to the Chinese mind. We recognize the authority of heaven, the authority of earth and the authority of human people. The Chinese consider man to be a new creation arising from the integration of heaven and earth, which means the joining of the spiritual level of energy and the earthly, physical level. People are the children of heaven and earth. We are the children newly composed of the spiritual sphere and the material sphere. We refer back to Pang Gu because there is no recorded history. If we trace back to the earliest stages of human history after Pang Gu, first the authority of heaven ruled, then the authority of earth and finally the authority of human beings. Heaven means nature. Earth means to have some knowledge about the earth, so that society can evolve. Then, human development produced the institutions of family, small community and large society. Following the development of human society, Chinese written history began. The first ancient classics record events that happened prior to the invention of writing.

In those ancient classics, we read about Sui Ren Shih, the one who developed the use of fire. I believe human life at that time was not much different from the lives of their fellow animals. They all ate flesh and blood. So, now a great leap in culture came with the discovery of using fire, which brought about the ability to cook food.

The second time or period of authority came with Eu Zang Ssu, the person who developed housing or a practical "nest." Before he lived, humans did not know how to build shelter for themselves. You can imagine that the living conditions of our earliest ancestors were very primitive. Through inspiration from the birds and animals, our ancestor Eu Zang Ssu, whose name means "the nesting start," created the first type of constructed housing. Before him, we lived in caves, but now we moved out to make nest-like houses in the trees or perhaps on the ground, and that began to lend a shape to the culture. Who was that ancestor? We do not really know. We only know that after a long period of living on the earth, humans began to have a capability to build houses by constructing a simple nest. Please do not think that today's sort of housing is the same as that of our ancestors. This was a long stage of human history, which lasted until Fu Shi.

Some classics mention that Fu Shi lived over 300,000 years ago, but this large number mainly represents a long period of time. Some Taoists believe he lived between 10,000 and 80,000 years ago. In ancient times, people depended on hunting; when they felt hungry, they went hunting and lived on the flesh of animals. Sometimes they had the good luck to find something to eat. They did not know how to store food, and the meat they ate could not be preserved. I believe that for a long time hunting was not difficult and there was an abundance of food. Then they experienced a new difficulty: sometimes they could not find an animal to eat for many days. Therefore, herdsmanship was developed by Fu Shi. This breakthrough began a new period of human life. The people did not need to rely on hunting, but could instead use the animals they had raised for food whenever necessary. The period of herdsmanship lasted a long time, but we do not know exactly how long. Even with today's human intellectual achievement, instruments and knowledge, experts still cannot agree about the interesting experiences of our past.

Anyone who lived then who had some special development, attribute or capacity was recognized as such by his fellows. Society was not very organized at that time.

Governmental forms such as monarchy are much later creations which gave rise to more difficulty than the natural way of life. Fu Shi was one such natural leader; it was he who recognized the difference between masculine energy and feminine energy. He made a symbol for the relationship of masculine energy and feminine energy which is the tai chi circle. He not only used this symbol to classify the masculine and feminine energy among animals, but he also applied it to describe the entire universe. Tai Chi, the ultimate truth, was conceived or shaped in his mind. The truth Fu Shi discovered was that in the oneness of the universe, the whole being of Pang Gu, nothing can be recognized. So, starting from the point of original integration or oneness, a great step forward is made with this recognition: the experienced universe is relative. The universe is two forces, creative and receptive, two ways of movement and stillness that assist each other and interplay. The entire universe, nature as a whole, any life being, society, family or even small particle of basic life or sub-atomic nature, has at least two great aspects, external and internal. It has two important, fundamental elements that interplay and work together for developing, moving and continuing life. Yin and yang are the names for these two forces. When the two forces work together, there is life; there is beingness. Once the two forces cease to be active, the life or sense of beingness is no longer necessarily expressed.

The discovery of these two forces was important. It was seen that neither of the two forces should be overly extreme so as to extinguish the other force. Each must find harmony with the other's expression; then they provide mutual assistance. A mature accomplishment creates one being, composed of the two energies, and keeps it in good shape and in proper order.

That was Fu Shi's discovery. But there was more to it than that: he developed a symbolic system to represent it. He saw that there were not only the masculine and feminine forces, but there is a middle, intermediary force too. He used three lines to express this objective understanding of nature. He continued to develop the three line or three stage combination of each individual existence by stating the eight different possible circumstances or combinations of the three. These were three-line symbols or trigrams. The eight circumstances and trigrams are also represented by the words heaven, earth, thunder, rain, wood or wind, mountain, fire and water. The names are symbolic of the energies represented by the trigrams; they serve only as examples. People who learn this system of symbols know it can be applied to many equivalent things, not just earth, fire, water, and so forth.

Fu Shi's discovery or invention of the symbol system represents one stage of humans starting their own observation of nature, their surroundings, themselves and their fellow animals. He put together a system that describes the universe, nature and general reality and the capacity of the human mind to interact with and control it. That was a great accomplishment. Fu Shi's hard work, and the study of his work by other people, resulted in the conscious or unconscious raising of the human mind. You see, the human mind is not separate from the human spirit. We could say that the development of the eight trigrams is spiritual inspiration operating through the intellectual function of mind.

The mind of Fu Shi objectively drew the first two symbols - a broken line and an unbroken line - to represent two different aspects or features of an existing situation. Then he continued to develop the eight trigram system, which inspired the system of Chinese written characters.

The ancient people tackled the difficulties of nature that affected their lives, especially weather changes, seasonal changes and the sun. They experienced the joy and happiness of life as well as the discomfort and depression of life. And they also experienced moonlight and no moonlight, which are reflected as hypertension and low or stagnant energy, respectively. The experiences of these two forces can be represented by the yang line (one point or one line) and the yin line (two points or a broken line). The lines also express the sun energy and moon energy. The eight trigrams can be used to represent the warmth of the sun with the four seasons and the light of the moon with its four phases. The broken line or two dots represent the new moon and the winter of the sun. My purpose is not to teach you how to apply this system, but to mention how the development of the human mind, interestingly enough, started from knowing how to use simple symbols. The observations that resulted in the symbols of the eight tri-grams came from many years and generations. The human mind has lived a long time; it is constantly being refreshed and grows through new experiences. But many, many generations passed before the ancestors were inspired to make use of symbols to express what they knew. That is interesting. The ancient people were much wiser than we are, because now we are educated to have a stiff mind.

At least we know that Fu Shi conceptualized and sym-bolized two concrete spheres, the yin sphere and the yang sphere. Yin expresses the weaker side or something more subtle. Yang means something more apparent or clear and strong. But each has its function and helps the other. Function connects yin and yang, because they serve each other as one unit. That is an important concept; do not neglect it, because in the future I will talk about it more.

To return to the story of our ancestors, Fu Shi passed on his position of symbolic spiritual authority to his sister's family. It was a time when human authority began to be recognized by ancient society, but it was still long before monarchy began. His sister's family maintained the stan-ding of Fu Shi's authority because his sister, Neu Wu, had an important supernatural achievement, the spiritual capa-bility of affecting the weather and stopping rain. That was the first time a person did something like that, or at least there was no previous record of having the skill to affect weather. The simple existing record only mentions who developed housing, who developed fire and cooking food and who developed herdsmanship. First there is a prob-lem, then the solution arises. Fu Shi's life represents a change in human evolution from living by impulse to living by reflection and contemplation. At that time, people also needed to know and understand where they were and what the truth was behind phenomena. This means that they needed to know the position of human beings in the universe and the truth behind their life experiences.

During the time of the great rain and flood, the woman leader, Neu Wu, who was believed to be Fu Shi's sister, utilized colorful stones to affect the rain. She created wind to disperse the clouds which carried the heavy water. This is a great spiritual practice. Surely it was her human spiritual power of conscious concentration that stopped the rain. Because of her the rain stopped, the flood condition lessened, and people enjoyed the normalcy of life once again.

By doing this, Neu Wu started her epoch of leadership and became the center of Chinese society. She was titled by people as the "Queen of Wind" because of her spiritually meritorious contribution of stopping the rain. She became the symbol of authority, but I do not think that at that time we would have applied the word "authority" to the person who was the image or center of ancient society. There are some old paintings showing a man's head and body, and a woman's head and body, with the lower part of the bodies like a belt, connected together. That was Neu Wu and Fu Shi. This depicts the transfer of social authority. She became the image of the center of society and used that picture to tell people, "My connection is with Fu Shi."

Human evolution came to a new stage during the time of Shen Nung. Shen Nung was the person who developed agriculture around 7,000 years ago. Some sources say he lived around 3218 B.C., about 5,200 years ago. From herdsmanship, humanity came to a new stage: the discovery of agriculture meant that people could use plants to sustain life. They could use many varieties of natural herbs and vegetation as healthy food for people. At the same time they looked for all kinds of nutritious food, not only vegetables, and recognized the medicinal properties and uses of different herbs to help cure specific problems of the human body.

After the period of Shen Nung, writing began, so historical events were recorded. The Chinese character system was initiated by Fu Shi using two different lines to express yin and yang. Before his time, rope knots had been used to record important events. The line system was the inspiration for the Chinese written characters in Shen Nung's time.

Shen Nung's tribe, the Han, continued the ancient cultural development, but in the same area there were many small tribes that were culturally and spiritually less developed. There was much danger, aggression and invading from the other small tribes which had slowly unified to attack the more developed Han tribe. The agriculturally based Han, whose center or leader was Shen Nung, was having difficulty with the increasing problem of the smaller aggressive tribes and a new leader, the Yellow Emperor, was chosen by the people to resist the invaders. The Yellow Emperor was chosen at the age of sixteen, because he was smart and brave and had excellent physical energy.

New inventions are important if people wish success in the struggle for survival. The difficulties of wartime especially require material advancement, so therefore, several important developments occurred. One of these was the simple weapon. Chinese medicine also became more organized during and after the war. Another important breakthrough in the war was the invention or discovery of the compass. Without a compass, it is not possible to find one's enemy or bearings in a heavy fog. The first compass that was developed was set on a two-wheeled cart, and one person pushed the cart around everywhere. He followed the tribe to determine the direction in which to go and to return so they would not get lost.

An English proverb says, "Necessity is the mother of invention." I believe that there is nothing untrue in that proverb. So the more developed Han tribe succeeded against the invading barbarians in this war for survival. The Yellow Emperor became universally recognized as the first emperor of a new society because of his leadership in battle and the development of the compass. This began a new era for the Han tribe. It was a long period of peace, prosperity and rapid evolution. The Yellow Emperor and his wise wife cooperatively developed many things. One example is his wife's discovery of the use of the silkworm's cocoon which grows on mulberry trees; thus, the first piece of clothing was made. Other clothing and special uniforms were developed incidentally or in an organized manner. That time period brought a great leap in human culture that has lasted close to 5,000 years. I believe now you can ask the question you already mentioned once.

Q: Are you sure you are ready? Did you give enough background?

Master Ni: I will continue. You can ask. I will still develop the discussion further.

Q: Thank you for this nice discussion. Your answer was interesting, but I guess what I am really asking is how I can deeply know my own soul. I do not exactly see how what you described about the human past relates to my question of now.

Master Ni: Your question is still too early because at this stage of history, people still did not know or have the need to look internally for the soul. At this time, they were interested in religion: the external worship of heaven. Is this not an illustration of "necessity is the mother of invention?"

You see, people used to live a simple life on the earth. At the beginning their consciousness had not yet grown. Before that, they must have had an emotional life, but they could not distinguish the source of the power that brought about all kinds of obstacles in their lives. After the consciousness of the human mind grew, they slowly recognized that there was something behind all the natural phenomena. Could there be a master or a monster who could make trouble like people do? If trouble were caused by a neighbor, they knew where the problem was and they could always fight with him to straighten out the problem. But they began to sense this force behind the natural troubles which affected them so much and they could not fight it. From dismay, due to recognizing their helplessness, a fear grew deep inside. How could they improve their situation? Their fear could be explained or eased by the older people in their tribe or race. This was the beginning of religious motivation. The other thing they wished to know was the origin of their ancestors. Was there some kind of master or monster behind all of this, or not?

One thing they experienced was that the ghost of their ancestors sometimes entered the weak body of a woman or a child, to tell them about an impending problem. The ancestors loved and gave warnings to their descendants, and the descendants loved the ancestors. The ancestors could not give a reason for the impending trouble, but they gave the warning, because human ghosts or spirits know what will happen. Although the ghost lost his flesh body or house, it could still occasionally borrow some weak soul's house to express love or concern for the descendants, or just to nastily express itself. So negatively or positively, the worship by shamans of ghosts and the worship by the common people of ancestor-spirits was developed. This is how the primitive tribes in China developed a kind of worship or communication between the spiritual realm of their ancestors and the flesh life of the descendants.

II
Shape the Unshapable

Q: Does the word worship mean to communicate with, or to honor?

Master Ni: Either way. Because the descendants wished to remember their ancestors, and the ancestors wished to be remembered, the rituals started. It is also interesting how the rituals developed. The descendants felt they needed to repay the ancestors, because of emotional need or practical reasons, so they made offerings and developed rituals of how to bow, how to offer, how to do this or that. It simply arose from practice; nobody promoted it. It was used for personal purpose, not to sell, etc. Nobody promoted that people do such things, but such human customs arose from practical life situations of needing advice or emotional help. In the beginning, it was just a tribe, a small family that lived together with only a mother; there was no father. Nobody knew who the father was -- please do not think this was wrong, but just realize how human people developed. There was no divorce because there was no marriage. Were they respectable people? I think they were respectable.

However, sometimes the male came to approach the woman, and maybe he attacked the daughter too. The woman and her sons and daughters united to beat the man and chase him out, out of hatred or jealousy or just out of an intuitive feeling of "not right." I do not think they had developed any intellectual knowledge about the danger of inter-family sexual relationships.

But because your interest is more related to religious and spiritual practice, I will return to discuss that. At that time, during the years after the Yellow Emperor, they had worship and communication, and they made offerings to the ancestors. Still people had no desire for the knowledge or the saving of their own souls. There was no question about that. They only felt the trouble and the possible danger in life. They needed some help. They had fear about the outer, natural environment. Especially during the struggles between two tribes, each tribe needed the help and guidance of their ancestors. So the worship of ancestors naturally developed in each of the different communities and different tribes. Such worship was popular in each tribe and developed naturally in each one, although there was no unification or contact among them. It arose naturally. I do not think at that time there was any further spiritual development than that.

It is interesting that before the Yellow Emperor faced the threat to the survival of the Han tribe, the main leader of the enemy tribes was Chih Yu. Chih Yu's side was knowledgeable; first, they wielded weapons made of metal, although not shaped metal, because it was just something like a stronger stone. Second, Chih Yu unified nine tribes who made him their leader. Third, he knew how to communicate with tigers, lions and other fierce animals and manipulated them as soldiers in the war. Fourth, he knew how to affect nature by making fog or taking advantage of foggy days. Nobody can see in the fog, and so the other side can be easily defeated.

Spiritual leadership is inherited by the spiritual energy of stars. The Yellow Route of the sun was divided into 12 zodiacal zones in the sky, each of which affects the choice of leaders. Long before, Fu Shi had been inspired by the Big Dipper and the natural rotation to outline the *I Ching*. His sister, Neu Wu, was also inspired by the Big Dipper which pointed to different directions and thus showed the seasonal changes. What she thus obtained was the power over nature. Thereafter, this tribe confirmed its spiritual relationship with the Big Bear constellation in the sky to include the Big Dipper and thus named itself "the Kingdom of the Bear."

The farmers who were the descendants of Shen Nung could not handle the invasion of Chih Yu's armies and the Han tribes suffered greatly. But in the Kingdom of the Bear, the son of the chief, the Yellow Emperor,[5] was elected at age sixteen to organize a group of young people to fight Chih Yu. The dates appear slightly different from various sources.

War is the mother of invention. War is the mother of a great amount of creative energy. War is the mother of religion. Sorry to say that! But it is reality; a new stimulation to the mind.

You may think we can call heaven, call God, call anything to come and help at a crucial time, but God is unshaped. Where can one find God? The smart ancestors looked to the stars. The first thing they recognized was that all the stars in the sky circle around the Big Dipper every year. The Yellow Emperor suffered one defeat in the war, and so knew he must win the next battle; when a person wins he becomes emperor, when he loses, he is a rascal. He knew that if he did not win, he would be slaughtered with the whole united tribe which was fighting the army of the allies of nine tribes under the leadership of the half-animal person Chih Yu. So he prayed to the Big

---

[5]who, according to one source, reigned from 2698 to 2358 B.C.

Dipper, which resides within the Big Bear. He was greatly inspired by it, and in his troubles, some of the older people were also inspired by his worship. So they did the same and all became empowered by this new reverence. In Chinese, this is called "Jiu Tien Shuan Yu"; in English it is translated as, "the mysterious maiden of the highest heaven is the transformed energy from the Big Dipper."

With this spiritual inspiration, the soldiers became unified, made the compass and thus had no problem in the fog. With a new knowledge of strategy, the Han tribes found the light of survival. Some might say that it was a material achievement, but I would say that it is a spiritual discovery.

The Han tribes believed human life connects with the spiritual energy of natural life, with the heavenly bodies. Each heavenly body, singly or in a group, has its natural energy. Once that energy is communicated to humans, it can make people really great, intellectually and physically.

So this spiritual connection won a great war for the Yellow Emperor and the tribes under his leadership, and made a peaceful environment in which to further develop a great, stable society of all the tribes, winners and losers together. Now both sides harmonized to live together despite their opposing roles in the war. Agriculture developed further, Chinese medicine was established, and clothing was improved. Nowadays, you need to pay a lot to go into a topless club. At that time you did not need to pay; also nobody offered you any strong liquid like they do now.

Q: I think you are making a joke.

Master Ni: People are so serious; you are looking for high spiritual seriousness, and me making jokes like that! It is not degrading, it is only that our vision has changed. By watching the sky, people become smart. By watching money, people become stupid.

At that time, nobody thought other people were sexy or not sexy, because all were natural. However, modern people can now know that we were helped by Heaven. For any achievement we make, we need to think of giving the credit for the help to our natural environment. The ancestors thought the entire sky helped them, the sky decorated with stars. This means the light. People are helped by the light, internally, subtly or apparently. The complete Heaven with shaped stars and unshaped spirit is our guidance. So the later human worship of religions organized by the human mind is not the natural heaven. Natural heaven never proclaimed itself, "I am God, so I can be dominant over all of you." No, it always yielded to any human creation, whether right or wrong. Heaven lets each human find its own correct growth. There is no single being called God. Heaven is not similar to the concept of a single being, a ghost or a spirit as God.

Among the small ancient tribes the people worshipped their ancestors and, in a unified way, people worshipped heaven as the spiritual reality of the entirety. Humans should never give up their position in the universe. We are equal to heaven and earth. We are the middle, we are the sons and daughters of heaven and earth. The expression of integral life does not mean that I can live and you must die; it means that I live and everything lives. It is an interesting and beautiful life. What we call Heaven is the entirety of life, impartially, without distinction. It means, the entirety of all existence and all lives. We find differences all the time, but harmony is what brings our lives together. Disharmony is what brings wars and destruction.

At that time, life was still sometimes threatened by nature, but humans did not yet need to turn back in search of their own souls. External worship was commonly practiced by ordinary people, but there was no type of religious dominance. The highest heaven represented all freedom; an all-embracing, boundless, endless authority. In this stage of human evolution, impartial heaven was recognized by the Han tribes and the other societies as the spirit of public service.

Do not hurry. I did not answer your question yet, because it comes stage by stage. You feel the pressure now, because the monster of society grows so strong. At that time, the monster of society or the government was minimal, so you did not feel that need. You were so happy.

Your life was so connected with the life of the universe and related to nature, why worry about your personal soul? But I will clearly answer your question as we go along. Have the patience to listen to me talk more about the Yellow Emperor, because he was one of those who initiated the Taoist tradition.

It was told that after spending nineteen years as emperor of China, the Yellow Emperor became bored with his life. People crowned him around 2697 B. C. Let me explain a little bit about the political system then. At that time, basically there was no political system at all. "Emperor" was just a name for a person who represented the center of society. You cannot use the idea of the emperors of western society like Julius Caesar or Napoleon to think about the Yellow Emperor. The Chinese word for emperor is Ti. At a later time, the position of emperor also turned into monarch which was somewhat similar to the western emperors; but that is still a different type of emperor than the Yellow Emperor.

You see, at the time of the Yellow Emperor, society and each individual practiced self-government. Each family, community and tribe was self-governing. The title of emperor is the word "Ti" in Chinese, which means stem, just like the stem of a fruit. I think the word Ti used to describe emperor, is a better, more respectful title in some way, much more so than the modern connotation of the word emperor. Huang Ti, the Chinese name for the Yellow Emperor, was just a symbol of the center of society, and thus he was popularly appreciated and respected. After he was in this position for nineteen years, or some say sixty years, he became bored. This young fellow now had grown older; there was no more challenge in his life. Life became so easy. I think occasionally he had to hunt for his own meat, but mostly people hunted for him. At least he had that enjoyment, but nothing else, I believe; no fancy car, no white house, no anything.

Now he looked at life, his own life and life in its broader sense. All life is so limited. What is the true significance of life and living? What is the correct way to enjoy life and to live a good life? The answer he was looking for was something that his highly developed teachers could not offer him. You see, in his position, he gathered all the greatest talent in the country. He, along with his advisors, originated the calendar, the system of sixty symbols that mark the different days, months and years. He had a teacher to teach him medicinal knowledge, one to teach him Chinese herbal knowledge and the way to prepare the medicine before they used concoctions. He had other teachers too. But after he learned all that he could from them, his vision, his focus changed. He began looking for something deeper and more fundamental about life. So he gathered energy and looked for helpers. Surely in his position he had helpers who told him in which mountains lived the great sages, the people already achieved in spirit. At that time, they did not necessarily use the word hermit to describe those people, because people stayed anywhere and so the mountains were just another place where a person lived. But almost always those people of spiritual achievement lived in the high mountains.

The Yellow Emperor traveled with his helpers and climbed the big mountains to look for the teachers. He found Guang Zhing Tzu, Giu Tien Hang Pin, and other men who were great masters at that time, and he collected knowledge from them. This knowledge now exists as so-called Taoism and if it has become a special school, it originates from the search for and the gathering of knowledge by the Yellow Emperor.

I will skip over the part about how he achieved himself. The reason is, if I do not do that, I become a kind of salesperson, because I am involved as one of the last generations of this school. His son was Shao Hao,[6] and his grandson was Chuan Zueh.[7] The biographical dates of birth to death are not known. Our family are descendants of his grandson. I also need to skip describing my ancestry

---

[6]who reigned from 2598-1514 B.C.

[7]who reigned from 1514-1436 B.C.

in detail; I should not say my great-great-great-great grandfather was the virtuous model of public service.

Then, after the Yellow Emperor, human history came to the time of Emperor Niao.[8] Emperor Niao was a wonderful person. He searched out and found all the spiritual teachers of his time, but he was not lucky enough to step aside to enjoy. During his time, the flood problem was a tremendous natural calamity for those who lived along the Yellow River, in the region of northern China. Because he had learned spiritual arts and knowledge, he wished to quickly find the right one to take over his responsibility as emperor so that he could fight the flood. Finally he found Shun.[9] His dates of birth and death are not known. Shun was a farmer. He was not loved by his father, mother or stepbrother. He had trouble with them, so he lived independently. Many people liked and respected him, and he gained in reputation by starting a community and teaching people agriculture, tilling and farming. Niao had heard of Shun's achievement, and he wished to find out more about him, so he gave his two dear daughters to him in marriage to see if Shun was as capable a leader and as creative a person as he had heard. He proved to be; therefore, Niao gave up his throne to Shun and instructed all his sons to follow Shun.

After Niao gave Shun this responsibility,[10] Shun needed to face the task of fighting the great flood problem which was growing bigger every day. So he found Yu.[11] Yu was the one who helped him conquer the flood, the water problem. I mention this, because there were many legends collected by a knowledgeable and wise minister of Yu, an old scholar. I have assigned some students to work on that

---

[8]who reigned from 2357-2258 B.C.

[9]who reigned from 2257-2208 B.C.

[10]at around 2,255 B.C.

[11]2205-2297 B.C.

book. I am interested in that book because during the
period from the Yellow Emperor until Yu, all of the leaders
were spiritually developed people: Taoists. All of them had
a Taoist spiritual association and had their own practical
teachers who helped their spiritual development. The helpers and advisors were all Taoists in that first stage. The
main feature of Taoist government or management is that it
allows people, each individual, family, community, location,
tribe, or town to have self-government. The central government role was only to gather capable people together for
solving specific problems. The emperors were the center or
spiritual symbol of society. They did not perform any particular religious customs, because each tribe and each
individual was allowed to be different. That is why I respect
them. Maybe most of the Chinese people are homesick for
that time. The Chinese culture of later times became very
bad.

   So when you meet Chinese people, they will be proud
of their ancestors and they worship their ancestors, remem-
bering the golden days with the open leaders who set an
example but imposed no real influence or authority over
Chinese society.

   Do you like this?

III
Imagine the Unimaginable

*Q: I still don't know how this relates to what I am trying to
do, the deep experience of my soul.*

Master Ni: You do not need to hurry. The question is how
and when do you start to search for the knowledge of your
soul. I am referring to "you" as the collective human consciousness, not "you" as an individual person. This is why
I need to give you an explanation. If I do not give you an
explanation, you will think it is your single personal pursuit. You will not know how it became a common pursuit,
how it became a matter of great confusion and how misguided the people came to be about this important issue. I
am not afraid of undertaking this lengthy review of the

history of human development. I would like you to get the whole picture, then the question will naturally be answered. Now let's go back. Because the people loved Yu for helping to save them from the flood, Shun naturally passed the throne to Yu at around 2205 B.C. Yu, however, did not pass his throne to his son. He passed his throne to one of his important ministers, "I" (pronounced "ee"), an outstanding scholar who kept a record of the campaign of fighting the floods, as they went all over, making channels that would allow the water to flow to the ocean. So on their trip, "I" gathered information about many people: their customs, religions and stories, and he recorded them in the book *San Hie Jin,* the *Book of Mountains and Oceans* . He was the one who received the throne from Yu. Unfortunately, however, people's attachments asserted themselves. They became attached to Yu's family, so they made Yu's son Chii the emperor. They neglected the one who actually received the recognition and bequest of the throne from Yu.

With Chii, China came into a new epoch, a new stage. This new epoch meant that the symbol or authority of the country and of society came from a family lineage instead of choosing the one most suited for the job. The king would be followed on the throne by his son and then grandson. This continued generation after generation, until Ji,[12] the last great-great grandson of Yu, who became corrupt after taking the throne. Tang,[13] an ordinary citizen, wished to free the people from this unjust ruler. He took the throne away from Ji by fighting and defeating him.

Tang and his helpers started a new government around 1766 B.C., but he followed the same custom of passing down the throne by family inheritance, until Jow.[14] King

---

[12]1818 B.C. (Note: It was not the custom to keep dates of birth and death or records of the emperor's personal matters in the public record at that time.)

[13]who reigned from 1766 to 1753 B.C.

[14]The last emperor of the Sarng Dynasty which lasted from 1766 to 1121 B.C.

Jow was a tyrant, so King Wen, who completed the work initiated by Fu Shi in compiling the *I Ching*,[15] laid the foundation for a revolution. His son, Wu, who became known as King Wu,[16] succeeded in accomplishing his father's goal. He started the revolution and ruled as the first of the Chou Dynasty 1122 to 249 B.C. During the Chou Dynasty, the minister Chou Kong Tang,[17] who was one of King Wen's sons, set up the service or ritual of marriage. That was the beginning of all the trouble.

As the act of people joining their lives together became formalized through ritual, thus initiating the marriage system, an artificial family order was established. The father had the first position, the mother second, then the rank of the sons continued down, with the elder son first, then the second. The highest position was always passed down to the elder son. The decision of who would lead the family was not made by selecting the wisest individual, it was strictly ordered by who was born first. If the first son died, the second son had an opportunity. What could have been natural flexibility in filling political or social leadership positions became limited by this cultural formality.

During that time period, however, monarchs did not have any special privileges, so there was no competition for the position. The only exception was during the time of war, but that was not often. So not too much attention was given to the situation. The great Chou Dynasty succeeded mostly by continuing the old tradition, the old society of self-government. It lasted 800 years. At the end, the leaders, feudal lords and kings of the small tribes started to compete with each other and also to compete with the central government headed by the emperor. So at its beginning, the symbol of the center of the Chou Dynasty was recognized as the emperor. But at the end, because of

---

[15]Around 1154-1104 B.C.

[16]1122 B.C.

[17]1104 B.C.

competition and rebellion, the attitude towards the emperor's position changed; and from being like the Yellow Emperor, Niao, Shun and Yu, natural leaders of the people, the position became the pinnacle coveted and seized through competition and rebellion. The central position of emperor became the target of competition among the feudal lords, and they warred with each other to see who was stronger and would be the leader. The ancient system of passing on leadership was totally disrespected.

Then came the time of Chun Chu,[18] which is called the Period of Spring and Autumn, and following that period was the Warring Time.[19] After the establishment of the family system, a similar system became steadily and consciously established in feudal government, consisting of a lord superior to a group of subordinate slaves. This then led to constant struggles over who was a slave and who was a lord. Let me tell you about one thing that I truly hate.

Q: Master Ni, do you have hate?

Master Ni: Surely, I have hate. It means I do not like something. At the time of the Warring Period, the feudal lords had power over everybody and could even kill somebody if they wished. In those times of severe confrontation, the formal mania of organization started to appear. When one feudal lord died, then all the women who had slept with him, and his servants and maidservants too, all had to be buried alive together with the dead king. I dislike that very much, but at that time it was an observed custom. Digging in the tombs of those old kings, archaeologists have discovered obvious signs of the many people who struggled to get out.

You are interested in finding out about the soul. Now we will talk about the soul. The soul means the substance of each individual life. You have the substance of your

---

[18]722-481 B.C.

[19]403-221 B.C.

individual life just as I have my own. In reality, it is not a single substance, but a group of spirits that forms one individual. When the group converges, there is life. When it scatters, flesh life is finished. Each individual being is composed internally of many smaller spiritual beings as well as different organs and systems which support the functioning of the entire human life being.

A life has many levels; life formed and life unformed are quite different. In human life, you can establish an artificial rank, such as "I am the King." In this way, whatever work needs to be done, if I am the king, I can find somebody to do it for me. So those of high rank can use those of low rank to do their bidding, mostly from ego need or swollen emotion. This is a sickness. Sometimes having things done for you is necessary, but if you overdo it, and create a system to support your distended emotion, that is really unfortunate. Although it is the tendency of the human mind to do so, it is not necessary, because when life returns to the much more subtle substance of life, a different stage is reached, and there is no required form. Once there is no form or shape, there is no practical need for food to eat, no need for clothing or housing. At that stage, there is no need for servants or sexual intercourse. Only people who are enmeshed in form and substance of all kinds feel the pressure for sex.

But at the time of which we speak, even though the dead king had no need of them, his wives, concubines and stewards were buried with him, a whole group of people there just to die for him. This became a custom. Custom is human made; it comes out of the human mind. The young king's descendants or his old king father thought it needed to be done. So there came to be a wide separation between the real truth of the soul and the human custom of religious practice which was no longer truthful or natural. Any knowledge about the soul, whether it be truthful or untruthful, can become the source of a new custom, and once a new custom is established, religious practices develop.

Today, if someone lives in Hong Kong and his mother or father passes away, he will hire people to make a beautiful house, car and kitchen out of paper, and all of these things are burned as a gift to the deceased. The custom, though it no longer involves human life and possessions, still continues, only the form has changed.

Q: You are saying that burning the paper houses is basically the same custom as burying the people.

Master Ni: Not only do they make a house, but human shapes too: a man, woman, present maids and menservants are made from paper to be burned too. This is the custom. You see how long human customs last. Not only do they do this in Hong Kong, but in Taiwan also. Have you seen the exhibition of the contents of the tomb of the first emperor of the Jing Dynasty?[20] When they found his tomb, they dug out a whole life-size stone army, with stone chariots and stone horses. There were hundreds of figures. That was one step further in the spiritual custom and religion of that time.

Now I hope you are not confused. I am not condemning past customs; they are only superficial. My point is that when a king thinks that after he dies he is still a king, this is totally untrue. It is not true that if you were an emperor, after you die, you are still an emperor; if you are rich, after you die, you are still rich; nor if you are poor people, after you die, you are still poor.

When a life in the human world, no matter what its social make-up, comes back to its natural substance, it becomes the same as everything else. All is oneness. It was interesting that in the Chinese monarchical system there was a king, a premier and all kinds of officials and ministers, and in their religious beliefs there was an upper world of heaven and a lower world of shadows, where there were also similar social orders of kings, etc. Their belief also held that if a person was good, he would be rewarded in heaven and if a person was bad, he would be punished by going to the shadow world.

---

[20]who reigned from 248-207 B.C.

In fact, the spiritual world is the reflection of the human mind. What a person sees depends on the maturity of his spiritual development, because the spirit world a person reflects is exactly the same as the image he holds. When human concepts change, the reflections change too. However, spiritual reality is basically similar to what they believed, in that it has three levels. About this, we shall have more to learn.

Concerning the Chinese customs, when I was a youngster, my mother and father once gave me instruction about the matter of burning those paper objects. They said, if we pass away, do not do such a foolish thing for us. But my sister said, if we do not follow this custom, I do not know if our society will consider us to be living correctly in the world.

I have made a big circle and now I would like to come back to talk about how the religions started. I would like to discuss the true way of spiritual cultivation that connects with your internal substance. From the time of the Yellow Emperor until the end of Chou Dynasty,[21] 2,448 years had passed. During this period of time, China only had spiritual customs, but no religion. Spiritual custom is produced out of daily life, with the addition of certain basic religious beliefs and rituals. But religion is much more organized, with doctrines, ritual worship, a history of each religion, and organizations and particular people who promote them. The old Chinese customs were not organized, but were later turned into a religion.

At the end of the Chou dynasty, scholars and achieved people responded to the sickness and disease of the current society by giving teachings to restore normality. For example, Confucius[22] wished to continue the practices of the ancient spiritual customs. Mo Tzu,[23] who continued

---

[21]2697-249 B.C.

[22]551-479 B.C.

[23]501-416 B.C.

the teachings of Yu, said that people needed to restore their faith in an impartial heaven and worship the benevolence of the spiritual world.

Let me backtrack for a moment; I have not given details about the Great Yu. When the flood was occurring in most parts of central China, the young, human minds of the people were faced with a great challenge for the first time. They had definitely exhausted all their sources of knowledge and capability. Spiritual practice or methods, which you might call magic, was one of their resources, because such tremendous work was needed to open the mountains and guide the water from the surface of the earth to the ocean. Remember that at that time, people lacked machines and modern knowledge. Their work was based on the use of bare hands, so they demonstrated great courage in their fight against the water, and they needed great help in facing the natural disaster.

It was the second time after the Yellow Emperor that a leader went to the mountains to gather important spiritual guidance for help with a huge problem, seeking instructions about how to live a healthy, natural life. The Great Yu's assignment, his mission in life, was different than that of the Yellow Emperor. In confronting this tremendous natural calamity, he went to the mountains to seek the wisdom of the hermits or, perhaps, those people just came along to help him with many kinds of spiritual practices and capabilities. Either way, he was the second one who went to gather effective spiritual practices and help from the natural source of direct inspiration of high heaven.

The Great Yu, by the way, was an example of unselfishness. After his marriage he took only one day off for a honeymoon. Then, he immediately left home to go lead the people in fighting the flood, day after day, night after night. He had no personal life. People came and went, some new hands came to help, but he was the one who constantly worked from the beginning. He set an example of diligently working for the benefit of the public.

So the life of Yu was an example of great achievement. His collection of spiritual practices was continued by Mo Tzu. Thus, the worship of impartial Heaven with many effective practices had a new life, a renewal. The later religion that became known as Taoism worshipped Niao as the Minister of Heaven, Shun as the Minister of Earth and Yu as the Minister of Water. Those three great people became symbolic spiritual authorities.

Q: So there were two floods, one solved by Neu Wu and one solved by the Great Yu?

Master Ni: I think so. The stability of earthly life, according to the ancient people, was not great at all.

Allow me. Mo Tzu's teaching was different than that of Confucius. Confucius also based his teaching on ancient spiritual custom. He used the examples of Niao and Shun as virtuous models for all people. Niao and Shun were kind, open and unselfish. Mo Tzu taught at an earlier time, but he lived long enough to witness the developing problem. He emphasized in his work that the problem came from cultural and psychological confusion, and confusion of spiritual vision, because people did not know what to follow. Meanwhile the dictators, small monarchies and lords competed for universal authority or dominance in the Chinese region.

There was another, older teacher, someone who was much older than Confucius and Mo Tzu. Lao Tzu lifted his voice to call for the people to come back to nature: "All ye who have lost your true nature and vision, do not fight for something untruthful." This is his voice. But he did not establish anything. Only later was a religion founded. A form of Taoism was begun which included the collection of spiritual practices of the Yellow Emperor and the Great Yu, some parts of Confucius' old customs and the teaching of Lao Tzu. Lao Tzu's teaching is the harvest yield from the study of ancient ways and history, particularly the means of harmonizing yin and yang, as initiated by Fu Shi and completed by King Wen.

Different practices developed from this base much later, one of them being the art of Tai Chi Chuan, which then branched off into many different schools. It is a Taoist principle to train oneself utilizing a form such as Tai Chi

Chuan or other such spiritual practices. It is a life training. It is not meant, however, that one give over one's life
to serve that form. Some students belonging to certain
schools of Tai Chi become biased and respect only what
they have learned, disrespecting or commenting unfairly on
other schools. Chinese calligraphy, for example, also has
different styles and schools, each according to the tempera-
ment and characteristics of the practitioners. All render
the beauty of the art; none is better than the others. People
do not fight over calligraphy, although they have preferences. Fortunately, preference for a style of calligraphy is not
enough to start a war, but with martial arts it is different.
Many practitioners of martial arts hold an attitude of con-
tempt for the other styles and sometimes needless fighting
ensues.

My point here is not to talk about learning calligraphy
but about learning religion. People learn religion for the
purpose of spiritual practice. Unfortunately, once an emotional attachment is built into a certain practice or religion,
some people fall into fighting for it or becoming martyrs for
it. The true purpose of practicing it, however, is to use the
training, discipline and form to help oneself to develop. For
example, each individual has spiritual energy which needs
to be directed through education.

Let me tell you how this happens. Spiritual energy has
no form. People choose a form or a religion to channel their
spirits, otherwise their spiritual energy would scatter. For
example, somebody has faith in Tao. He carries this spiritual guidance and its healthy discipline in his mind. He
always retains an image, of Master Lu for instance, deeply
imprinted in his mind. Or he uses a picture of a spiritually
achieved one to concentrate his faith. He might also dream
of the achieved one. It is not that the achieved one comes
to visit him in his dream; it is his own spiritual energy from
his own good practice and strong faith that projects the
spiritual image of the face of the achieved one.

In many religions people worship statues and pictures
of a holy person. Is that picture the true face of the holy
man? Surely it is an artistic creation. I do not think the
artist has actually seen the holy man. But when a person

continually confirms his belief in the holy man, and looks at those pictures, any dreams he has of the holy man come from the spiritual image formed in his mind by looking at the pictures. This is utilizing an external form to regulate one's spiritual energy, and is an example of how spiritual energy may be channelled.

Similarly, Chinese people have faith in one deity or another in the shape of a majestic man or woman. There may be hundreds of thousands of pictures or thousands of statues of such a deity. The faces on the statues of the deities are different from those of the paintings. All are supposed to be the same person, but each has a slight difference because it is the work of a different artist. When people who have faith in such a deity find themselves in trouble, they use its image for help or inspiration. Does the deity come? No, it is the spiritual energy of the individual in trouble that starts to be active at that time. This is just an example.

Surely all religions have the images of sages. The effect of the belief in a religious personality is to shape your spiritual energy. People need to choose the image that fits their psychology. They may prefer one or a few or all of them; one's choice depends on one's spiritual sensitivity and response. This is the spiritual truth at one level. One God of many names is also different people's projection.

All beliefs and all religions are an external form. If you wish to use the external form to regulate and to channel your spiritual energy, it is totally alright. But if you think that the form you adopt is the best form, and you fight, reject or destroy the other forms, this is an expression of human emotion. It is not real religious service. Just like Chinese calligraphy, religious forms or images are tools for communication. At their highest value, they bring about achievement in the person using them. Whatever you use to mold, regulate or train your own expression of mind will bring about the corresponding result. The mind has no shape. You shape it, and after the training, you produce something similar to a type or style of art.

If you are wise enough, you can see that all religion is a shape, a form, a program. If you would like to adopt a religion, nobody can say your choice is wrong. However, you cannot say you would like to use your energy to promote only one form or style, and replace or destroy all the other styles. That is the danger of narrowness, stiffness and rigidity. My purpose is not to talk about the evil of religions. My purpose is to broaden the vision of ordinary people. I would like you to totally and thoroughly understand the function of religions and know their correct employment in human culture. If it is your choice, you can use one of them to be your model. If you are not satisfied with them, you can create your own meaningful practices as a student of Tao to maintain the spiritual flexibility and elasticity of your life and to embrace the wholeness of life, inside and out. So according to the function of your spiritual practice, you can decide what kind of image to use.

Most importantly, since we have been discussing saving the soul, I will speak further on that subject. Until you make your choice of practice, your soul has no shape. In the spiritual knowledge of my tradition, one can transform oneself into any form that one wishes, even a bridge, road or mountain, or a person of any age, gender or appearance. Such achievement can bring about one's freedom, though this art may now be lost.

IV
Transform the Transformable

Q: I would like to know more about spiritual transformation.

Master Ni: All right. We experience transformation from babyhood. Slowly each year we transform ourselves. Each five or ten years you can readily observe the change in your external form. Even a sage cannot escape the natural power of transformation. For example, many people have faith in Jesus. What part of Jesus' image do they affirm? When he was a baby, a student or a carpenter, a teacher, a martyr or an ascended one? You cannot say that only the baby is Jesus or only the man on the cross is Jesus. The part of the image of Jesus that a person affirms is the one he decides is the true image. Each minute of his life, he was Jesus, but each person confirms only a certain aspect, such as what is seen in a painting every Sunday at church. The painting seen in church is an artistic rendering and thus is different from the true Jesus. Whose image, then, is attested? However, the exactness of the image is not important. What is important is the sincerity of the student.

Therefore, it is important to learn wisdom from the spiritual source. Do not only learn the form. Today, people fight because they are not dedicated spiritual students. They only learn the form. They do not understand that no spiritual language can accurately describe the spiritual realm, because language is limited. A person must not shallowly believe that words are the spiritual reality itself. The spiritual reality is far beyond the words.

Unfortunately, many people have not attained spiritual development, so today there is more confusion, not only for the youngsters, but for adults who use their strength to fight for what they have never truly understood. Achieved people stand aside, away from the fighting, because they are already beyond that stage. Usually the achieved ones prefer not to be main characters in the world drama any more. So through my teaching, I wish people to make better spiritual progress, and to recognize the dwarfed, inflexible conditions they have created for themselves from their prejudices, partial ways of faith and unquestioned belief in myths and stories.

Positively speaking, for the one who wishes to do spiritual cultivation, your personal image is the best. I do not suggest that you must be self-loving in the sense that your image or face is better than another's, but you need to respect the way nature created you. All form should be respected for what is inside. The external form is just the wrapper. For example, a diamond can be put in an ordinary container. Surely an imitation diamond can be put in an expensive container, but the main thing is the reality of what is inside the container or wrapper.

So in your spiritual cultivation, look upon yourself as a fresh life. We also have some recommended metaphoric images, like sang ching, the three realms of purity which are the cover art on my first three books in English (*The Complete Works of Lao Tzu; Tao, the Subtle Universal Law,* and *The Taoist Inner View of the Universe*). However, they are only images. Sang ching is an illustration of the three spheres of your spiritual reality. But if you would like to use them, they will have a beneficial effect. Also, a person learning Tao can visualize the picture of Master Lu, Tung Ping as a way to channel spiritual energy. He is seen on the cover of the *Workbook for Spiritual Development of All People.*

In spiritual cultivation, the process of channeling one's spiritual energy is important. Once you can channel your spiritual energy to create a certain image, you can later develop many other ways to transform it.

My friend, I have already started, slowly, to touch the center of your question. I have pointed out that you must have faith in something. The faith, the creed you choose, and the content of your faith become part of your spiritual being. Spiritually, you are formed by that faith. I have shown you the guidelines in the last chapter of *Attaining Unlimited Life,* the book of Chuang Tzu. That would be a good faith; absorb it as part of your life being. Surely it may become your spiritual being.

I can give you another illustration. If you climb a steep rock-face, you need a reliable rope. Before you depend upon that rope, you need to examine it. Did other people tell you the rope was strong, or have you yourself checked it out? If you have any doubt about its strength or integrity, do not pick it up as your lifeline. Otherwise, in the middle of your climb up the cliff, because of self-doubt, you will lose half your strength. The contact of faith must be strong; and it must be consonant with your intellectual achievement. You cannot put your intellectual mind aside and pick up something that totally conflicts with it or with your own goodness or that makes no sense to your personal spiritual faith. If a person does that, then what is taken up becomes only psychological application, a sugar-coated poison. So you must choose something reasonable that firmly integrates with your understanding; that will be strong help.   Otherwise, as with general religious experience, it will help you at a certain stage of your growth, but you will eventually have to give it up for something higher or better, because such activity does not connect totally with your soul.

Most religious leaders know nothing about spiritual reality. They might have faith in what they can psychologically catch hold of, such as emotion. Life, however, is nature and it does not need the decoration of human religious make-up. Some people waste time with religious practice because they need a transitional emotional aid. Some people are so deceived by worldly influence or empty religious teachings that they completely divorce themselves from their natural soul and establish false beliefs inside their beings.

The second thing I mentioned is to have an image to concentrate on, to help you converge the subtle substance into one whole. I mentioned that some useful images are the sang ching (the three purities) and Master Lu. I also mentioned that the best one is your own image.

In the tradition of Tibetan Buddhism, students visualize the teacher's face or body, which serves the same purpose. Tibetan Buddhism and Zhan (Zen) Buddhism in China, Japan and Korea are organized for enlightening students; they offer laypeople a psychological bridge. One shortcoming with Tibetan Buddhism is that the student relies on the teacher to make each step of progress. If the teacher does not say something, the student can never be enlightened. If with each step of the learning journey, a student needs the blessing of someone else, it is a religious ritual. Then the student needs the enlightening words or further instruction from the teacher. Those people who become lamas (Tibetan spiritual leaders) spend their whole life following a teacher. The teacher does this to them, and they do the same thing to their students.

Enlightenment is a precious thing, but a lot of time is wasted because religious truth can be so openly known. How much time a person needs to spend depends on his spiritual maturity. Spiritual independence would be gained at too high a price, if to come to that stage, the student has to spend decades and become old before the teacher speaks the truth about the religion.   In that case, his enlightenment might be to finally discover that the whole system is just educating foolish or ignorant people, the people who need someone else to channel their minds.

Zhan (Zen) Buddhism is different from Tibetan Buddhism. In Zhan, the students also need teachers, but they are more open. Students can wander from one teacher to another. Why? Zhan (Zen) Buddhism also teaches enlightenment, but the students are not allowed to rely on the teachers; they must rely on themselves. Maybe the teacher will give them a subtle hint, but it is up to the students to achieve themselves.

I would like to tell a story about achievement of a different kind. Maybe it is a joke or a metaphor. A father was in the business of lifting things from people's house; this means he was in the stealing business. His son was now of the age to learn from him. It was his family's tradition that if the father was a thief, the son would also be a thief. Each walk of life, you see, has its own special training. Usually they worked together, and the son learned from the father.   One day, after several years, the son asked the father, "Can I leave and work on my own now?" On that day and on many other days the father answered "no" to this question, and the son would say, "I'm doing all right now. You can let me go off on my own." Finally, the father said, "Okay, but first I need to give you a test. If you do well, it means I have taught you everything.   I am concerned that you have not learned everything from me. You do not need to urge me to let you be independent. I have been waiting because I have not yet passed my total knowledge down to you. So we will wait for the right opportunity, and I will teach you the last special secret."

At dusk one evening, the father and son sneaked into in the yard of a house. The son went inside the house and the father remained outside.   Usually, the son would go through a window and hand the things out to his father. The son began to work, first checking that everybody was sleeping, but just when he started to collect the valuables, his father threw a brick at some empty metal garbage cans, making a terrible noise. Then he walked away.

A light went on upstairs, the people were awake. The son, inside, thought surely he would be discovered. Quickly, he went over to the window and began to make a noise, "Meow, meow, hsssss, hsssss." A moment later he heard a man's voice, "Honey, it's just those darn neighbor's cats. Go back to sleep." The light went off, and it was quiet again.

When the people of the house went back to sleep, the son finally got away safely and came back home. "You crazy old man!" he said, "How can you set up your own son like that?" "I am not the least bit crazy," the old man replied, "Now I have taught you all that I know!"

So if you come in contact with a really good Zhan (Zen) master, this is what he teaches: you need to learn by yourself.

Neither the way of Zhan (Zen) nor the way of Tibetan Buddhism is my way. In my way, I give you everything. You do not need to search for enlightenment, because there are still many strenuous efforts to make if you wish to achieve yourself as a realized person. It does not mean that it is too early for enlightenment nor that groundwork is needed before the search. Neither the tools are available, but require effort to use for achievement. The truth is apparent. The energy of an individual person is not strong enough to see it.

Now I would like to give you the third instruction about saving the soul: remain in quietude. You can do meditation, but meditation is only one way. A quiet life is important. An exciting, disturbing or confusing life with all kinds of mixed up maneuvers cannot be followed well by your soul energy. Only when you stay in quiet, centered within yourself, can you one day gather the subtle elements to be united with your physical life being.

Speaking broadly, after the death of an ordinary person's soul gathered in the body, part of the subtle substance stays in the tomb, part of it is scattered everywhere, in the trees or on anything with which it comes in contact, and part of it goes to the descendants or anyone related to the person. It totally loses the independence of being.

A student of Tao, however, engages in spiritual practice and quiet training and learns to be independent, so when that moment arrives, he is centered. The yang energy, the life energy, has been gathered, and the subtle substance does not scatter. Then anytime, if you wish to form yourself, the spiritual energy can gather as some form, whatever form you like. If you wish, you need not bother with the human world. You do not need, without good reason, to respond to anybody; you can disappear.

Many achieved beings remain living; within my reach there are many. This is not the teaching; it is just to say there are beings that stay in an invisible stage of beingness. They can appear and disappear. Even though they are invisible most of the time, they exist and they are alive. They do not need to pay rent or taxes or rely on anything. They do not have any worldly restrictions or restraints but enjoy great freedom, because they are achieved and at a different stage. They relate to students, they enlighten people, they help people if they find someone worthy of help.

So this is the third instruction: keep quiet or be quiet. There are meditation techniques, of course. The most important meditation technique is being centered without falling asleep. It is not mantra, it is not sutra, it is not visualization, it is just to awaken. You keep the sense of awakening within; that is the best centering. In the *Tao Teh Ching*, that is called the mystical castle or the mystical point.

Q: The mystical pearl?

Master Ni: The gathering is called the mystical pearl, but the sense of awakening is called shuan kuan. Kuan is called the mystical checkpoint or castle where all people need to pass through. The front of the head could be called the mystical harbor or mystical port, like an airport, a spiritual port. That is the extensive function of shuan kuan.

In a spiritually developed person, it serves as an antenna to receive all signals.

Now we can move from this point to see the fourth. Let us talk about how much or what length of time is allowable or suitable for our daily activities and what endeavors are suitable for a person doing spiritual cultivation. Because this connects with the techniques of cultivation and the purpose of the cultivation, I will tell you about it when we discuss the techniques and the purpose.

Q: You were talking about meditation. Sometimes when I sit, I feel energy collecting at the top of my head. Should it do that?

Master Ni: It is all right in the head area; the head area is better than the sexual organs. The energy center for the sexual organs is the lower tan tien which is the center of the lower abdomen. Only old men or old women, whose sexual function is already drying up, need to pull energy down there for the purpose of rejuvenation. However, once you achieve being able to move your energy there, do not destroy the achievement by extending your interest to the doing of sex.

You need to be more centered, pull the energy to the point between the nipples. Be centered there, behind that point. This is for all young men and young women. Young to some means before 50 and to others, before 30.

Q: I did that in the past when following that instruction. It creates a lovely feeling, of the heart center opening, and all the lovely feeling comes. It makes you feel bliss, a kind of joyous, peaceful happiness that is different from the happiness of excitement. If you keep it there, you feel bliss all the time.

Master Ni: My tradition teaches women to be centered. Among men, it depends. The heart area is the center for women and older people. But generally, there is a further instruction for higher spiritual cultivation. This level is the foundation. Continue to follow this principle. Do not play with this energy, but quietly watch it. Never use thought to twist it to be something else. Once it is gathered, nurtured and becomes strong, you can guide it to make a small circle, then a larger circle and then larger, clockwise 30 times. Then make a circle as before but counter-clockwise 30 times. It can be 8, 12 or 24 times. For the serious student, this is to channel your sexual energy and refine it into chi, then to transform it into sen in order to facilitate attaining spiritual immortality.

Q: So it is not helpful to collect it at your head then?

Master Ni: You can feel energy on your head; energy can move anywhere if you are not bothered by it. If you feel partially congested, it is a problem and you need to use energy-guidance conducting to subtly gather it in the center.

Q: You mean move it away and then regather it.

Master Ni: No, it does not matter; just do not have any congestion anywhere or in the head.

Q: Yes, sometimes I do, if I have to think too much.

Master Ni: You need to move your energy back when it becomes congested. If thinking causes congestion, look down at your feet. The front center of your feet we call yung chuan, the fountain point. Letting the ascending energy come down to the front part of the center of the feet will restore your peacefulness. Sometimes the energy itself is rising on your scalp, as though you were wearing a hat, or you may feel you are sitting in a beauty parlor getting your hair styled. If you feel that way and it does not bother you, that is okay. If it bothers you, you can gently look down as I instructed, gazing at your feet. The energy will come down to restore the natural flow again.

We learn in our tradition that if you overdo sex or other things, you will not have that kind of energy, so you will never feel it. You need some basic training of moving your energy to clear up congestions. For that purpose, we have groups of movement called the Eight Treasures exercise. You may also mentally rotate the congested sexual energy in a circle around the center line of your body. This practice is described and illustrated in the *Workbook for Spiritual Development* as the "Great Outer Circulation."

Q: What about the orbit circling?

Master Ni: That is another basic method. It shows you one of the ways to move the chi cyclically. Few beginners have the feeling of chi, but many people pursue it. However, orbit circling is for serious students who have stopped sex, wishing to manage their sexual energy but not force it as does kundalini practice. In general, it is not necessary that somebody visualizes or artificially does this.

If you are sensitive and you feel that the sexual organs are becoming congested, there is something you can do before the energy changes to sexual fluid. You can do the circling before the energy which is in that moment is still not liquified. By moving it away, it can be retained and stored as chi in the body. Some people will feel chi congestion every day in the sexual centers of their bodies, so it is a good practice to do the circling every day. Sometimes, after trying the orbit circling, a young person's sexual energy is still too strong. Then it is better to do some other kind of movement that avoids concentration on the lower tan tien. In this case, the complete circle should only go as low as the navel. The circle can be big or small; it can be from front to back, and it also can be from left to right. There are still better ways. But a young person needs to avoid moving the energy down to the sexual organs because the energy is easily stimulated when we are young. This makes it hard for one to control one's life, and one will do something improper. One needs to have the complete knowledge when doing such a practice.

Q: If I do the orbit circling, is it done by using the mind to guide the energy? I have read something about that, but you said not to do it, that it was for older people.

Master Ni: Never make a mental exercise out of it. It is not a mental exercise. If you feel the energy staying in the ocean of your sexual organs, then move it away. If your sitting position is not right, the energy will not flow well, and you need to move it away. If the energy is congested in the head, younger people should not move it down to the sexual area, but move it to the limbs by gentle exercise. Once the clouds move away, it is a fine day.

Q: If I practice Chi Gong physical exercise, and I come in the house to start to cook breakfast, all of a sudden I notice that breakfast doesn't come together very well. I wonder if I should stop doing chi gong.

Master Ni: (Laughs.) I believe you have found the wrong time. You should do chi gong around half hour or one hour after eating and then start normal activity. Because the exercise you have just done makes the chi flow a different way, you may cook differently, and the food, the smell, the way of cooking and use of the flame will all affect your work.

It is excellent to know something about cooking. Internal movement can be parallelled to the way of cooking. Food can be cooked too much, not cooked enough, cooked by the wrong method such as frying in heavy oil instead of lightly steaming, seasoned for better flavor, and so forth. Chi practice follows the same principles you use when cooking.

Q: Is it that I am doing the chi gong wrong? Or maybe I am not gathering ...I haven't learned how to gather the energy at the end of it well enough, and I am still scattered?

Master Ni: No, it takes time to become excellent at managing it. But I still think you need to set a good time interval after doing chi gong before you come back to ordinary daily life.

Q: Do you mean just do it for five minutes at a time until I learn to handle it better?

Master Ni: Do the whole series of exercises, then rest for half an hour or an hour or do something else light. In that way, you will manage it.

In ancient times, people practiced tai chi chuan or chi gong but lived an ordinary life. Those people stayed in the married form of life or family life. There is a regulation about how to do things without hurting your energy. It is called "Three before and four afterwards." It means three days before you have sex, you should stop practicing your cultivation. It means you stop all tai chi or chi gong, or any exercise practices associated with chi for three days. After sex, you do not exercise for four days, then you can start your practice again.

Young people are always up and down. They build a little bit of energy, then they lose a little again through sexual indulgence, so they are always in that bad cycle. They feel they need to do it. But afterwards when they are achieved, sex is not interesting any more. Because when you practice, you need to practice every day, no matter what kind of conditions are present. Naturally, dedicated students find out sex is of no benefit, because when they do it, it hurts their energy.

There is a certain special practice to enhance sexual pleasure, but it is only for a period of fantasy in your life-time. In the long run, it is not the right direction.

Q: That leads me to the question of my menstrual period. It keeps me on a yo-yo, up and down.

Master Ni: There is a practice among Taoist women called chan chih leong; it translates as "kill the red dragon." To kill the red dragon means to stop menstruation. I do not seriously recommend that today's Taoist women do it. In ancient times, because Taoist women lived like men, nothing different, they used that practice once they attained spiritual achievement. The only difference in spiritual practice between the sexes was the inconvenience of menstruation. Women would decrease it, then slowly make it go away totally. It is not a recommended practice for all women. Older women starting Taoist cultivation might need to use herbal medicine to make menstruation come back. People can become old but they must be complete when they do the cultivation of Tao.

Q: The women used to lead the same lifestyle as men?

Master Ni: They could live as men and do the same spiritual cultivation as men. They had a problem with their periods, so they developed a special practice to stop menstruation. The reason that I do not recommend this practice is that those lady Taoists lived in a natural environment without the external temptation of having undisciplined men around. Once they controlled themselves, the energy would not flow down to their sexual organs any more. Today this would be difficult for women, except those who are devoting their lives to attaining higher spiritual achievements.

I recommend that serious students, women as well as men, do the traditional golden immortal medicine practice. tion, or not enough orgasms would lose their balance of mind, or even become mental patients; so they engage in sex or otherwise they perhaps become eccentric.

To serious students, I recommend women, as well as men, do the traditional golden, immortal medicine practice. Each morning, when the man's sexual organ stirs naturally, the man would be benefitted by getting up to gather the energy back to the center. Otherwise, if the man stays asleep, he will have one of several problems: he will have sexual dreams, unconsciously masturbate or have nocturnal emissions. This practice of gathering the golden immortal medicine is practiced by both men and women. They do it at midnight if awakened by sexual disturbance and anytime. Modern medicine thinks these things are natural, but if you are serious about gathering your spiritual energy, you will do this practice, because sexual energy is what supports your spiritual energy. Inside the sexual fluid is the chi, the subtle energy. The fluid is not 100% important for your spiritual cultivation; it is the invisible chi, the subtle element in the sexual fluid, that one does not wish to lose. That is the most important thing.

So people who overdo sex surely cause the loss of sexual fluid, but more damaging is the loss of the subtle chi, the subtle energy. This is a discovery of this tradition that occurred over long years of practice and refinement.

For a woman in menstruation, the real loss is not the loss of blood. Before the beginning of your period, your body starts the descent of the energy and at the time of menstruation, you release and give out the congested blood with that energy, speeding up the process of physical maturity and aging. In other words, your energy begins to descend several days before your period begins. When the period starts, the chi is also released and given out. It is a loss. Menstruation speeds up the process of physical maturity and aging.

Therefore, I suggest that both men and women in serious discipline do the traditional golden immortal medicine practice. Every morning, when relaxed and the man's sexual organ stirs, the student needs to sit up and do this breathing. First do strong breathing, then gentle breathing, to conduct that energy back into your body and back into your center. Every day you gather a little bit; every day you gather a little bit more. Then after long years, the so-called golden medicine is possible because of the daily gathering.

Once I was shown a newsreel of how opium is produced. It is also a process of gathering. Opium comes from a small bush that grows a fruit like a small potato. Every day they gather the white fluid from the opium fruit by using a bamboo knife to make a little break in the skin of the fruit. By the next morning it excludes a white fluid. They use their fingers to gather the white fluid in a porcelain container. They gather it in small quantities until it fills up the whole bowl. After they refine it, it becomes black. This is just to describe the process of the gathering; it happens little by little and you are not really aware of the accumulation.

Through this type of accumulation process, every day a student gets a little bit of the immortal medicine. Without external stimulation, women are not stirred up every day like men are. If there is external stimulation, then there is difficulty. When females are teenagers, at midnight the sexual organ will become hot and jump, so the woman will often use her hand to press it and cause masturbation. However, if you do that, you damage your energy of youthfulness. You become mature faster, but this is also self-damaging. At that time of sexual pressure, it is important to do the same practice as men do: get up, move the energy away which has congested there creating the disturbance. This is an important time.

The special term for that time of day is "Hou tzu shih," the flexible tzu hour. The true hour of the beginning of the daily solar cycle is always at around midnight or 1:00 a.m. "Tzu shih" means midnight, and the beginning of the body's day is at that hour. That hour is important; take advantage of it to do this practice. It is the same process, first strong breathing, then gentle breathing, to refine the energy into immortal medicine. The effective practice for youngsters is to go into the fresh air to do chi gong, tai chi or sword practice as spiritual exercise.

For women, the most important loss is at the beginning of menstruation when the chi is released, not the loss of blood or the lining of the uterus. Another similarly important occasion is ovulation. They are two different times. Loss of chi does not happen at once. Those two special times are important for women. They become sensitive and emotional when the energy comes down and disturbs the general balanced beingness. They must be smart enough to do daily cultivation, especially at midnight, and at the time before ovulation and before menstruation. When the energy is naturally descending you need to arrest it, refine it and transform it into your golden immortal medicine.

To continue with the example of the opium fruit: opium is good medicine for stopping a cough or diarrhea, but it is a bad thing for people addicted to it as a narcotic. Similarly, when you know how to use your sexual energy properly and not abuse it, it can be helpful to your cultivation.

Q: Sometimes when I sit quietly in meditation, the muscles of my sexual organs or anus involuntarily contract. Sometimes I feel warmth in my legs. I do not "do" these things, they happen to me. Sometimes nothing happens at all. My meditation is rarely the same each time. Is all that okay?

Master Ni: It is all right to experience physical and mental phenomenon. It is important not to let yourself be carried away. Then there is no problem.

Q: I usually am busy and not sensitive enough to notice when my ovulation occurs, but I do notice when I get crabby. So should I stop my activities at that time? When I begin my menstruation, I am not always at home quiet.

Master Ni: Yes, it is difficult for modern women, because their life is not a quiet life. The same is true for most of today's men. They are always maneuvering on the highway, at the telephone or in the office, making contact with people. So this is why a student of Tao must take advantage of the energy at midnight. If you do not have a quiet time during the day, at midnight you cannot get up because you are too tired. In general, if you wish to have a good, quiet meditation, you need to nurture your chi. Otherwise your chi is bad and you cannot get up; you are too tired and there is no substance to support you. This is why a quiet life is the foundation of spiritual cultivation.

Today, most people just ask that I give lectures, just give knowledge. When you realize that your cultivation depends on what your environment allows you, you make the best adjustments. I cannot give any specific instructions to stop you from shopping, driving and doing things. I can only give you a specific, simple practice which is that, subtly, gently, use your internal eye to look at the middle point between the nipples. That will help to keep the scatteredness from happening too badly. Also, gently watch your breathing.

So to start with, live quietly when cultivating Tao. That is a blessing. I do not think young people value that blessing; they like to be too active.

Then any time you feel an important hour, when ovulation or menstruation happens, follow the instructions I am giving now. Do not use tampons, they hurt your energy by sucking it out; use a pad instead. During ovulation and menstruation, no matter where it occurs, it is helpful to avoid engaging in any vigorous physical activity or emotional confrontation. At that time, I believe it is better to remain yourself and restrain yourself. There are certain things you should not do, responses and decisions that will need to be postponed, reactions that would best be delayed. Make your excuses to your surroundings; say something like, "Give me a break, I need some time to respond to this."

Q: Several times when I had a really quiet life for a while, I was able to be really centered because my life was not too active. I would sometimes wake up at 3:00 a.m. and feel a very gentle, sweet energy coming into my head. Is that important?

Master Ni: It is a good sign.

Customarily, young people need to be somewhat active in their lives rather than stay alone too much, so that they can build an understanding of the world and learn how to take care of themselves in modern society. If they rest or stay alone, the first thing that they notice is their sexual energy. That usually makes the person, man or woman, start thinking about the opposite sex, perhaps to the point of becoming frantic. Then the thoughts will slowly build up, suggesting that they take action and go out to look for a partner or else the thoughts will drive them crazy.

This is why I offer books and practices to my students to use and apply in their daily life, rather than send them to monasteries or something similar. I wish them to learn self-management in all kinds of situations. The most important thing is self-management. At different ages and in different life stages, one will feel varying degrees of difficulty in managing oneself or managing different aspects of oneself. I would like my students and friends to learn self-management, so they can manage their energy in all circumstances. A person who stays alone might have too many sexual thoughts. Listen to good music, but do not listen to love songs that tend to make you more emotional or fantasize. Do something more creative, more benefitting for yourself. Never allow yourself to be alone with any tendency that is self-damaging. It would be better, in that case, to be social, to be around other people and offer help. If you do not have anything to do, help others accomplish something.

Q: I am not sure I understand how your answer relates to my experience of the energy coming into my head at 3:00 a.m.

Master Ni: Oh, I have already answered that it is a good experience. In cultivation, a person has all kinds of experiences and that is one kind. A person whose energy is good might have that experience in a quiet life.

People who are too active will not feel that they have any energy. But on the other hand, can people who live a quiet, solitary life manage themselves well? A person might become sentimental about loneliness. Many strange behaviors and improper attitudes brew inside lonely people who do not know how to take advantage of the great opportunity of solitude to achieve themselves.

V

Q: I want to tell you one of the methods I used in the past to help me with my cultivation. I had a job in a busy office and they played the radio all the time, those sentimental love songs on the popular stations. Instead of listening to them like ordinary love songs, I made an association in my mind to remind me of my cultivation so I could keep my awareness at the point between the nipples, as you always tell us. So every time I heard the songs on the radio, they would remind me to center. This is how I was able to keep my balance in the middle of a general worldly environment. That helped my cultivation a lot. So the songs did not bother me in an emotional way and I was able to use them to help my spiritual cultivation by guiding my thoughts.

Master Ni: You are smart. Many things in the world are not necessarily beneficial but you can see how to apply them. In my herb room, as a Chinese doctor, there are all kinds of poisonous herbs, but they are useful medicine if applied correctly. In the same way, magazines like Playboy or Penthouse, or pornographic magazines are not for young people. They are for people who are over 150 years old, whose sexual energy has already died out, so that maybe the flesh memory can return and the person may find some physical revitalization.

Q: I know we have to be really careful if we do a practice like associating some external thing with spiritual cultivation. If one associates or puts a spiritual connotation on the wrong thing or something that is harmful, he can cause trouble for himself. But that is not my only way of practice. As you always recommend to us, I live in a safe, quiet place and lead a quiet life, apply myself to my job so I can do it well, and am mostly uninvolved with worldly things, such as TV and socializing.

Master Ni: All experience makes you strong, makes you sturdy. It is better to live a worldly life and become achieved, than to live in a bottle and become achieved. This is always my recommendation. If you cloister yourself in a nunnery to become achieved, it is not safe once you are out! It is better to live in the world, to expose yourself to all kinds of temptation, changing fashions, handsome boys, delicious food and everything, but ultimately to not be bothered by them because you have grown beyond them. If a nun depends on unintegrated, imposed discipline, it is not totally reliable because it is only an artificial restraint.

I myself do not have experience in turning love songs into a reminder of spiritual practice, but I do have the experience of turning love melodies into a sweet spiritual melody when I do sword dancing practice for spiritual purposes. Also, sometimes I use love stories as metaphors to illustrate and teach the unification of the two spiritual elements.

We have talked about the fourth guideline of living a quiet life and conducting cultivation in quiet meditation or sitting. Now if you do not have any other questions, I am going to the fifth subject, which is movement.

When you go on a meditation retreat, if you have a special secluded place and can afford to stay there quietly for a while, you need to make a slow shift during the first one or two weeks from an ordinary lifestyle to a quiet life. Your psychology, emotions, physiology and everything needs this slow shift. Do not shift quickly. If you make too quick a demand on yourself, it will harm the body and your meditation will not go well. Make a slow adjustment until you enjoy the quietude and seclusion, until you feel the energy coming back and feel the place and the house with its surroundings giving you support. At the beginning, you may not feel it. Slowly, slowly enter the concentrated cultivation.   You should not make a sudden shift; that is harmful.

It does not matter if your retreat is long or short, but I do not think that modern people can afford to stay for a long time in retreat. Sometimes three days, sometimes one week, sometimes one month, several months or half a year. When you leave the quiet meditation and quiet lifestyle to return to a normal speedy life, you must give yourself some preparation and allow a gentle shifting.   Otherwise you cannot take it, and it will also be harmful. If you can, in both a normal lifestyle and in retreat, live a life with a certain amount of activity. In that way, shifting from either type of lifestyle will not be too difficult. Even if you stay in a rural place, keep active by doing all kinds of necessary house care and maintenance, all kinds of errands. In that way, it is easy to manage yourself. Otherwise, you will have so much time and so much quiet that you will not be able to make use of it beautifully. Do not be too ambitious and unrealistic, thinking you can switch channels immediately like on a television set. You are not like that; you need to know your mind, emotions, body habits, routines and so forth.

You ought to have a special purpose for your retreat; otherwise the retreat would be useless, only a punishment to a generally active person. One purpose is just to restore your nervous system to a better condition. Or the retreat may be for reflecting upon your life so you can have a better understanding of all your relationships and the things you do.

If you are learning a special technique, you have to learn from a real, experienced teacher. Do not imagine that you can do something like this by trial and error. A teacher who has real experience and has done such cultivation in quietude picks out the method which he thinks will fit you. Otherwise, it is not productive. Even in spiritual cultivation, we have different goals that have their own particular kinds of practice.

Today, we are all intellectually developed. We can take advantage of this to organize our schedules better and document the real effects of our work. Keep a record each day of what you are doing; a record of yourself. Even if you do not like to put a lot of time into writing down what you are doing, you can have a simple record of your achievement after a period of practicing cultivation. In that way, you do not waste time.

However, cultivation for some people is more of a waste of time than staying in the world and working. To people who are not ready, it is negative.

There are many spiritual practices and each takes you to a certain stage. The knowledge of a special day in the solar or lunar cycle, with a particular purpose, will bring about a specific achievement.

A very busy life or excessive lifestyle will disrupt the ability to have or use your own spiritual capabilities. If you wish to nurture your immortal medicine, you need time, special training, and to be at the proper stage to stabilize it. In a busy life these requirements are sometimes obstructed. Surely your cultivation is every day, every month, and over a lifetime, but you need to establish it in quietude at the beginning. An occasional retreat to concentrate and do that will greatly enhance the effect. Power can be lost too, when you come back to ordinary life.

Some people wish to have healing power or to have supernatural power over nature. These things can be learned, but it is necessary to have a goal or it might turn out to be unproductive, negative or fruitless, or just another psychological trip.

Q: Could you kindly tell us what are the higher spiritual goals, the spiritual accomplishments that would be helpful for the world?

Master Ni: Spiritual cultivation has many levels.   What I have given in my lectures and written in my books, such as *The Uncharted Voyage Towards the Subtle Light, The Footsteps of the Mystical Child, The Gentle Path of Spiritual Progress, The Way of Integral Life,* and so forth, is mainly for worldly consumption.   I am slowly moving to teach spiritual attainment at other levels, as I am doing now.

Now let us talk about how much movement we need during our retreat of full time cultivation.   There are two types of cultivation.   One type is sitting as we engage in different kinds of breathing or non-breathing, each kind with different purposes and functions, such as the developing of self-control and the controlling of vitality.   The other type is the many kinds of cultivation practices associated with movement.   Those movements are specifically designed to help your energy or to help your spiritual symbolic movement.   They need to be especially learned, because they are usually secret.

Taoism is totally different from the other practices, because it is not a self-taming or self-subduing system.   It is a self-generating, self-improving, self-developing method to achieve yourself from a natural stage to the supernatural stage while allowing you to live in both stages.   Yoga or Tibetan Buddhism have hand postures that can give you a kind of self-suggestion.   Yoga, however, does not express or teach the practical posture methods related to communication with the spiritual realm.

Certain movements constitute good practice.   Some movements should absolutely be avoided.   I would like to talk about that.   A man or a woman who does spiritual cultivation, especially the golden immortal practice employed in conceiving your red baby, at a certain stage cannot use a knife to cut animal meat or anything else in the kitchen. I believe for those things you need a truly experienced and achieved teacher to show you what can and cannot be done. A red baby is a spiritual being conceived as a result of spiritual self-cultivation. See the *Workbook for Spiritual Development* for more information on the red baby. Because most people have not deeply experienced spiritual learning, I will give you some general guidelines. If any movement causes a disturbance of mind or spirit, avoid it. Also, avoid any movement that upsets your energy flow, including the eating of any food that would cause an upset. Also, avoid contact or meeting with someone when it would conflict with that purpose. All aspects of life need to be put under your control according to the guidelines of spiritual mystical conception. It is the means to conceive your spiritual baby.

The most favorable movements for a person of spiritual cultivation are walking and tai chi. Unsuitable martial arts, like those associated with fighting or killing or sports that promote a similar level of consciousness will pull you down. The principle is that what you practice will become your achievement. So, spiritual people would rather do chi gong or energy conducting, Dou-in, rather than do any type of martial art that has the psychological component of combat. Daily work like gardening and household chores also has a beneficial effect.

All I have said here is an answer about the reality of how to help and nurture your enhanced soul. Your soul needs to be further developed. The most important thing is to enhance your soul for its ultimate freedom and independence. Usually, weak souls are eaten up or enslaved by strong souls.

Therefore, the way of spiritual development is not fit for general religious followers. These religious followers are weak souls. The reality of religion is a big iron lid which suffocates the organics of the soul, or it is a machine for soul-eating. Mostly believers are affected psychologically; it is not a spiritual teaching at all, but since they have weak souls, a weak psychology, they fall into the trap of becoming somebody's psychological victim. Most religions are psychological schemes that use spiritual terms and borrow a spiritual system. You need to be careful and watch out.

The next point is: is it best for one's life to be single or paired when doing spiritual cultivation? There are different spiritual cultivations, so different ways can be considered. When you are young, while you are doing some cultivation, it is not suitable for you to meet your girlfriend or boyfriend or contact with people for general things because you need to keep your energy quiet. For a certain time period, maybe you should not see anyone at all because dealing with each person means dealing with different energies. Or, during that serious period, limit your contact to only one person who is also cultivating with similar instruction. Have at least one room or one spot that is your special place for solitary cultivation without any interference, intrusion or interruption.

Generally speaking, if you are living alone and if you are already linked to the spiritual realm and have achieved the hearing of subtle voices and can see the subtle images, you can attract subtle beings, which are achieved souls at different spiritual levels, ancestors, achieved ones and pure spirits from different stars. The super beings will come to visit you. They come because there are no other people there. It is not that they are afraid of people, but they do not like the energy of ordinary people because it is not refined. If you have reached that level, then it is more beneficial to stay alone.

But if in ordinary cultivation, you do not particularly wish to make that kind of contact with the spiritual world or if you do not have that kind of capability or necessity, you can stay with a man or a woman for spiritual company, usually the opposite, or the same sex in a small group. But it is better not to be sexually related. Too much sexual relating will cause you to disrespect each other. You respect each other because whoever stays together with respect can engage in development with good concentration. You do not bother the other person with how much growth you have and the other person also does not bother you with how much growth he or she has, but there is the fundamental underlying connection that both of you are psychologically, emotionally and spiritually at least 75% agreeable. If only 50% agreeable, it is hard. If only 25% agreeable, you may stay one day, but you cannot bring any positive mutual help or mutual benefit to one place. That type of relationship is best avoided.

You can observe from married couples of the non-spiritual sort who stay together on a superficial level, that the relationship is hardly real. People all change; these changes are subtle and you may not see them. Perhaps, as a not too serious suggestion, the marriage certificate issued to a couple could be for four years, like the term of the American presidency, and as the president can be reelected for another term, so the couple can be remarried every four years, if they wish. The four years could be designated as follows: the first year to get to know each other, the second year to fight, the third year to adjust, and the fourth year to decide whether they would like to renew the agreement.

If they have children, it is best for them to stay together and both need to exercise great tolerance for twenty years. Why? Because you have a responsibility for the youngsters you bring into the world and cannot discharge it by giving them damaged psychologies. Marriage is for children, not for sex. A couple can appreciate each other, but to be willing to help each other is mostly a spiritual attitude. If they do not come together for spiritual cultivation, maybe it is for business, material or emotional needs.

So now I talk about spiritual company. A man and a woman have different capabilities. In some cases the man has more life force, by this I mean he has already provided for his material needs, and some women have the capability of maintaining a house, and the two can help each other without sexual involvement. Let the man have more time to do his spiritual cultivation, let the woman feel secure, contribute her time to their work and engage in her own spiritual learning and cultivation. When both partners are in individual self-cultivation, then the combined higher energies of the two can help to create a healthy, growthful environment. That way is ideal.

However, I see that at a more serious stage, in certain cultivations, one may need a helper. If they help each other and respect each other, and still have independence, I think nothing is wrong with such a situation. If they become sexually involved, and the energies get confused, then it is not a spiritual arrangement, and it is beyond what I should talk about.

VII
To Live a Life Flowing With Nature

Q: How do you go to sleep? Somebody once told me that Taoists cultivate all night long.

Master Ni: Everything is Tao. Clothing, eating, transportation, housing, education, recreation, family life, working, friends, politics, economics, all things, anything related with life is Tao. It means that anything done properly then meets Tao. Anything done improperly is against Tao. Anything done properly that has a constructive result is Tao. Anything done improperly that damages normalcy is against Tao. Therefore, Tao is followable and Tao is useable. A Taoist sleeps and wakes up too. It is one way to realize the principle of tai chi with yang and yin sides. Rest and work, awake and asleep, doing right sleep is a cultivation. A Taoist sleeps with the entire nature of earth. A Taoist awakens with the sun still climbing on its way to the horizon.

You are asking about how to sleep. My answer is that going to sleep and getting up is a specific art. To a mental worker, to someone like us, it is an important subject. To most physical workers, this question would be a joke, what art to falling asleep? When they go to bed, they sleep like logs; they probably could not wake up if they needed to. But if you want to learn the art of a conscious life, you do not live in a mechanical way, but live a whole life. If you want to get up early with a fresh spirit, you need to sleep well. If you wish to sleep well, then in the late afternoon and evening, you already begin to put yourself in a quiet condition, subtly, gently nurturing your energy. Going to sleep and getting up are a tai chi; they cannot be separated from each other.

The late afternoon or evening is not a time to see new people, visit new places or go to operas - I am sorry to say that to the people in the opera business. If at night you are excited by seeing an interesting show, your staying up late and getting up late will disorder the desirable normalcy of your life. In the long run, it is not beneficial for your health. However, we are talking here about the natural normalcy, not about the "normalcy" influenced by the later culture of human society. In natural normalcy, in the late afternoon or evening, you would best remain inactive. Do not be overactive and do not excite your mind. Spiritual energy, or psychic energy, is associated with the mind. Once your mind calms down and becomes quiet, you give your physical strength and nervous system a needed break.

To natural people, sleep is a refreshment, a time of fixing and restoration for the next day's functioning, and it is vitally important. Those who look deeply at spiritual cultivation, view day, including the afternoon, as a time to labor or work on many things, and night as a time for rest and restoration. It is a cultivation, it is a cyclic pattern of regeneration. Without a good night's sleep, the next morning as you continue to follow the routine of life, you have not restored your life being to a balanced condition. It means your bank account is getting low and, if you continue to do that, you will create overdrafts. Then you will have bad credit, and even bankruptcy can occur - that means you are sick and dying. So sleep is a natural help, it is the natural system. It is Tao. Tao is nature. The natural cyclic movement gives all life time to rest.

Some people need to make their eyes feel tired, otherwise they cannot fall asleep, so they sit and watch television or read a book. Some people just sit in front of the television set for several hours to enjoy the shows or the movies. However, that is not the spiritual way. If the TV story or the book is bad and if you are a sensitive person, you pick up all the bad energy which goes into your mental system as unhealthy, unbeneficial fodder. You may have eaten a bad dinner, you enjoy the poison dinner (some food is poison, you may not have noticed that,) but it is all absorbed in your nervous system. If you feed yourself bad stuff, it will affect you most at night, because at that time you are relaxed and receptive. To one doing spiritual cultivation, it is important that the evening be serene because impressions from what you absorb will affect your dreams.

All of this is why I say that going to sleep is an art. You have to be selective with what you feed your body and mind. Peaceful, good music is appropriate. Music that is too loud or disturbing is not fitting because it stimulates you too much. Gentle walking or comfortable chatting with pleasant company is also nutritious or beneficial. If the company is not comfortable for you, even if it is a close friend, your life companion, spouse or children, it might be best in the evening to go into your room or someplace where you can be quiet. If chatting with uncomfortable company is your daily routine, you will retain uneasiness and unpleasantness. As you go to sleep, you will carry that with you. It means the possibility of introducing an unhealthy element into your nervous system, your heart and your mind. If you are wise, you will find a gentle way to withdraw from this and go to your room and rest. However, even if you do chat with pleasant company about things not disturbing to you, it is still beneficial to be quiet a while before you go to bed and to withdraw from everyone to quiet yourself down from the busyness and the responsibility of the day.

Gentle music and quiet activity prepare you before you go to bed. You need to nurture and brew the gentle feeling of sleepiness before you go to sleep. This is a cultivation for sleep. First put your mind already in sleep, then you will sleep well. If you lie down right away, your mind will not sleep; nor will the sleep come soon. If you already feel sleepy and you have the signal of body sleepiness, but you get to talking about something, the feeling of sleepiness will then blow away, like leaves in the wind. It is best if talking is avoided.

I cannot talk about this subject without mentioning the food you eat several hours before your rest: your dinner. Some food can cause you much difficulty in falling asleep. We are not necessarily talking about stimulating, spicy food; even food that is too hot or too cold will make your body work harder. In order not to overtax your body, the nutritious food you have prepared should not be too cold or too hot. With regard to taste, it is better not too have it too spicy or too salty. Before you go to sleep at night, it is not advisable to drink strong tea or coffee. Even citrus fruit or any fruit juice that contains strong acid can cause an astringent reaction on your nervous system, a kind of tightness that will make it hard for you to go to sleep. However, eating patterns are usually a person's strongest habits. To be a Taoist, to be a student of natural life, one of the first things you learn is to liberate yourself from being a slave of unhealthy worldly habits.

So in the evening, quietly withdraw to your room. There are a number of invocations in the workbook that you can practice. Some are absolutely not fit for nighttime practice. But others are helpful because they are very gentle. You can recite them to replace the thoughts, confusion and disorder produced in your mind by the day's activities. A mind is not easily purified. In your daily contact, work and stimulation, contamination keeps occurring and cannot be eliminated unless you do something about it. Otherwise, it is as though you were playing an old tape, or an old record, over and over again. So in the evening time it is beneficial to recite the instruction for masters, the customary spiritual instruction. That is beneficial; even if you lie down, you can still do it. Then gently fall asleep with those good instructions.

Form a good habit; before you go to bed, urinate and empty your bowels so that you can sleep more comfortably and without interruption. It is necessary.

Some masters do not have much time to do formal sitting, some even do not like formal sitting at all. So how do they cultivate themselves? They use sleep as an occasion to make the tiger and dragon have intercourse with each other, taming each other within. That means creating a special situation of harmony inside so that the vitality does not grow old; it is always in good shape through this process of regeneration.

The secret of Taoist cultivation does not lie beyond the purpose of regeneration. If you can accomplish it in sleep and in everyday life, you do not need to do any other special cultivation in a specific way. But to be a true student, first learn some basic practice, then whatever situation you are in, you can do it. We say that it is healthy to go to sleep before ten o'clock. Do not lie face up; it is not advised for women or men. You might like to cover yourself with a comforter or blanket that is not too heavy or too stuffy. It needs to be light so that you can breathe. You are not being buried, you are going to sleep. Remember, your skin is a breathing system, if you stop it from breathing, harm is done.

Some internal diseases like cancer are caused by improper sleeping or by taking in food that is more than your body can handle. It all turns out to be a problem when your body rejects it and pushes it to one place and the place becomes damaged. This is why the body needs your trustworthy management, so damage does not happen. It is inexcusable to ask the doctor or the insurance company to manage your life; you need to learn all the details of how to manage your own life!

So when a Taoist goes to sleep, it is also a cultivation, a restoration. It is equal in importance to the daytime, when you make money and have fun.

One more thing: it is better to sleep alone, unless you have a special purpose. If you are not going to seduce your girlfriend or boyfriend, it is better to sleep alone, because after sleeping, the body may radiate negative rays which are harmful to the other. Using a big bed with different comforters, or sleeping in different beds in the same room is the healthy way. Surely young people have lots of fun in bed having sex, finally tiring each other out and feeling like a couple of dead pigs. In that way, each night you kill yourself a little. It happens among healthy, natural lives, but it is not what I promote or suggest. I have just described my personal knowledge about it.

So you ask, when do you have sex, make love? That is a different thing, and we will talk about it at a different time. Now I need to concentrate on this matter of sleep. If you sleep singly, sleep well. It is most important to sleep on your side. The most favorable side is the right side because it does not press the heart. Surely you can roll over and sleep on the left side also. The main point is not to permit stagnation of your physical being or energy flow when you sleep. You always need to allow a little movement, but let the moving be unconscious. How do you manage to move unconsciously? This can be done because in the afternoon or evening, before you go to sleep, you have already become inactive and the body has enough energy to turn itself over during the night. If you become physically exhausted, then you sleep like a dead log; it is really difficult because you have lost all consciousness. That is sleeping like a slave. It is not your own sleep, you have lost your mastery. You may not be able to manage your sleep well all the time, all year around, because sometimes you have to work hard or are on a trip. But when you can, I would suggest that you do it. That is my knowledge.

So now you have fallen asleep, in the first part of night, into what is not really deep sleep. If you have dreams, they are just the dreams that bring you to sleep, that is all; they are not important. At midnight you might have two kinds of conditions: some people have dreams and some people have rested enough. The dreams are sometimes a message from your own mind, telling you what will happen or what is good and bad. They are not ordinary dreams, they are your vision, your spiritual energy starting to be active.

If you are spiritually strong, you will awaken if another strange energy has entered the room and your spiritual energy is alerted. Or you may be awakened by the energy cycle at midnight, as it provides an important time to practice spiritual self-government without the interference of illusory dreams to block the clarity of heavenliness. Then afterwards, you can go back to sleep, but follow my instruction: do not sleep face up like a corpse.

If during the night someone has a nightmare, it is forbidden to turn the light on immediately to see the person's face. If your sleeping companion has a nightmare, you must not suddenly turn on the light and shake him or her. In the dark, gently call the person awake, to restore him or her spiritually to normal order. If you turn on the light or yell, in that moment a spiritual disorder may be caused and the soul may not return to the right spot; maybe the person will go crazy or death will occur. That is the ancient knowledge.

In ancient times, people in full-time cultivation did not go to sleep again after midnight. They remained in sitting meditation until the next morning. Then, in the early morning, they started to be active. It is hard for us to sit for so long and sleep so little, because to take care of our worldly life we have lots of obligations and things to do, so we go back to sleep until a desirable time to rise, around 5:00 or 6:00. This is the way we should do it. The adequate length of one's sleep is from seven to eight hours for most people.

So you have had enough sleep. Now you might ask me again, since you are a human being, when do you have sex? If you are truly serious about your spiritual cultivation, my recommendation is to avoid sex if you find that you are not strongly desiring it. If you have sex, surely it is preferable to do it in the early evening, at a time when it will not affect your normal sleep. There is a lot of knowledge about doing sex; for example, doing sex for fun, as a medicine, for energy adjustment or to have children. If some people do not have sex, they become crazy; so they need to find a healthy way to do it. However, remember when you have sex, there should not be any disturbance in your mind. A peaceful night with moonlight or starlight, not a night with a storm or strong wind, is best. Do it in a correct location, not too close to a cemetery or some place like that. If your purpose is to have children, it is especially important to watch those elements; otherwise you can never have a healthy baby with a bright future. Never use aids or stimulants. You may do well at sex or not. Mostly it is another art, but for the purpose of spiritual cultivation, it is not suitable to take your focus away from sleeping.

Now we come to the next morning. Morning time is so important. If you need to get up and you cannot, immediately put your hand to the back of your head and scratch it; scratch it, and do not stop until the energy fully rushes to your head. Do not stop until you get up and dress. Waking up is also an art.

I have mentioned that when you go to sleep, let your mind be the first part of you to fall asleep. Conversely, when you wake up, let your mind be the first to wake up. If your body is still in sleep, you need to scratch the back of your head, or any part of your head, to wake up the whole body. Once the energy is rising to your head, the whole body will easily and peacefully come back to the correct awakened order. When your life is light, your sleep is light and your waking up is also light. Otherwise it is all hard and you struggle. The moment when you wake up is so important. If you do not awaken, what do you do? You fall into the dream state. Dreams take away more of your energy than your daily work. In Taoist cultivation, dreams are energy which can be controlled to support your work on immortality and spiritual achievement.

Therefore, it is better to wake up early, before 5:00. If your mind wakes up and your body is still asleep, many different dreams may occur. In some dreams you see a vision of what will happen later that day. Because the human brain is so powerful, it can foresee things that will take place and know what you are going to do. But even those dreams are not beneficial. What is better is just to get up before any dreams begin. If you cannot do it un-aided, buy a timer and put your tape player on it with the lousiest music you have. Do not use a pleasant tape but do not use rock-and-roll. Use some reasonably good music, but a lousy machine and a lousy melody which will get you up to turn it off. That is still more beneficial than lying there dreaming.

A spiritual teacher or a person of spiritual cultivation who is growing spiritual energy usually finds that the spiri-tual elements wake him up. If you are already a person of such stature or credentials, there is a group of fairies hel-ping your life. The fairies are not strong enough to help you physically, but waking you up is no problem. They wake you up but, unfortunately, even if you become used to it, one day you may feel tired and find it hard to get up. This should create no problem, because your intellectual development has produced support for the fairies who could not always wake you up on their own. So you wake up with the tape recorder sometimes instead.

To spiritual students, it is important to have the experience of those fairies coming to you in dreams where you can see them when you are half awake. I am only saying that the experience is important; I do not think it is correct to rely on them.

So this is how to wake up. People do not like to wake up if they do not have anything to do in the morning, so they wake up late and make the newspaper part of their breakfast. Those breakfasts with the newspaper could cause people to have ulcers, but they may take that risk because they have nothing else to do.

When you get up early, it is important that you cleanse yourself. If you can, meditate for a short while to center yourself, then do some spiritual practice for a short while to gather together all the spiritual elements. There are lots of important and powerful practices in the workbook, though they are on a gentle, subtle level. You can recite those, they are helpful. They are really useful to help you to longevity and a healthy life.

The most beautiful time to walk outside is the morning in the golden hours before sunrise. Taking a little walk is okay, and so is playing in the garden or back yard. You need to get out of your room, if it is not rainy. If you live in a rainy place, it would be ideal to have a big house with a leakproof roof and enough windows for adequate ventilation. It can be almost like outside, although, of course, you need to adapt to the reality of the situation wherever you live.

Choosing places to live that are the most beneficial to human health is an art called Feng Shui or geomancy. Practically, geomancy is the choice or selection of your living environment.

I have generally answered your question about going to sleep, the art of rising, and getting up to use the golden hours to do your spiritual cultivation, if you can. If you know some Chi Gong or Tai Chi Chuan, early morning is a beneficial time for you to do these.

Q: Thank you kindly for your answers. You mentioned yesterday that a person who does a retreat should do so with a spiritual goal. Would you talk about some of the spiritual goals and which ones are worthy?

Master Ni: There are large spiritual goals and small spiritual goals. I have already gently suggested a few, but ordinary people do not know the subtle sphere. It is not until they have had the experience of subtle connection to the subtle sphere of the world that they become truly serious. So you need to develop your eye and your ear. For most people the ear is easy to develop, but for some people it is easier to develop the eye. The most difficult is to develop the entire body. This takes longer; it is the whole body responding to everything. It can be learned.

If I have time, I would like to talk about the achievement of the ancient masters. For example, spiritual goals. What troubles you most? Does your life trouble you? Well, then, first you learn life. You need inspiration. Pursue that inspiration until you totally understand. That means: is there trouble or have you made trouble? Or is there no trouble and it is only your projection or illusion? Or has your swollen ego made the entire world mistreat you and you do not recognize that you are the one who has mistreated your own life?

It is not I who need to say it, but what troubles you most? When I was young, I was quite different from other youngsters. At that time, I did not trouble myself. I only wished to learn something higher than martial arts, higher than the military power of the modern nation. At the time of the Japanese invasion, Japanese weapons and military equipment were better than what the Chinese army had, and we experienced defeat. So I wanted to look for the fundamental law, or the fundamental, most powerful thing in the universe. At the beginning, you see only triumph or failure in the battlefield, but later, step by step, you see that the winner is the loser and the loser is the winner. The true triumph comes when you are totally achieved.

In the business world, you make lots of money, but you do not see that you pay for it in a subtle way. You are encouraged to do more and more and so you continually lose more of your self. It is not until your finger is burned by the fire that you might stop. Maybe it is a blessing to be burned, because it makes you look inward for something else. I am not encouraging people to become negative by doing spiritual cultivation. I promote a balanced life, never forgetting one side or taking the other side too heavily. If you enjoy material achievement, do not forget your spiritual achievement. If you enjoy spiritual achievement, do not forget to provide for your material needs. In doing your spiritual cultivation, do not make yourself a nuisance or burden for someone else.

Q: This is a practical question. You mentioned elsewhere about never spitting out one's saliva. What about mucus?

Master Ni: Mucus is different; it is discharged because some part is physically wrong. You might have some inflammation or energy stagnation in your throat or have a cold and the mucus gathers to fight the external invader.

Q: I not only have some during a cold but have a little often during the day.

Master Ni: Always swallow it; any internally produced energy should be swallowed.

It is interesting to see how little the ancient people relied on food. Instead, they relied greatly on natural energy. They regarded all the fluids of their bodies as part of their treasure, first extracting the essence then eliminating the residue. It is a different conception from that of today's people. Today's people eat a lot and then make gas a lot. Ancient people ate little, digested fully, and seldom made gas. If they made any gas, they still thought about how to utilize the heat of that gas to regenerate themselves. No kidding! Nor did they cry. They considered tears part of human energy, and used that energy in a positive way.

Q: Did the ancestors sit a lot or were they active people?

Master Ni: Oh, they were active, happy people. Sitting came sometime later because people were overactive and hard to control, and they needed to look for a balanced way. Also, in teaching, some formality is needed to guide people. For example, in the temples you see the statues of Buddha sitting quietly, a symbol of quiet meditation. When you see them, they give you a feeling of inner peace, so the statues of Buddha are worthy of respect. Just as the image of people in physical movement for creative and beneficial work is respectable, so is the image of people in spiritual concentration or quietude. Worldly life is the interplay of movement and quietude. We can still consider the image of Buddha helpful. You might put a picture of Buddha in your house or room as a reminder of your spiritual cultivation. The picture will give you a feeling of quiet and calm. Creating an atmosphere is one of the psychological arts all religions use.

I myself believe that it would be beneficial for all people to be open to the creation of ideas, regardless of the tradition that produces them. What were the beneficial creations, such as spiritual immortality, contributed by all of the ancestors of the different races? All people come from one source, one nature. Nature is our grandfather and grandmother. We cannot deny it. We can unite to protect nature, respect nature and respect any natural inspiration given to the human race that brings about beneficial creations.

Q: Yesterday I talked about using music to bring out the feeling of bliss in my heart. In Taoist terms, what does that mean?

Master Ni: It is not just a feeling. You gather the good energy there, the light energy; then you feel it. Continue to nurture it. Do not be coerced or controlled by the feeling, but understand the feeling to see what to do about it. You need to nurture this kind of feeling; do not stifle it.

Q: When I was living in another town I had a spiritual experience I have been wondering about. One night, after a

*period of cultivation, I began to feel different, and all of a
sudden, in my chest I felt an intense energy moving in and
out, first stronger then weaker, for maybe ten minutes. At
first I thought I was dying.*

Master Ni: A woman must protect that part of her body
from invasion by the external spiritual world. Better still,
grow and protect your own energy.   There is spiritual
knowledge about how to nurture and protect it. You can
use an invocation and a spiritual practice.

I believe it was a natural experience that you had at
that time and that you felt it because you lived quietly. It
was a natural flow of energy. You just did not notice that it
was still consistent with Tao. I believe that experience was
guidance for you so that you might know the direction in
which to nurture yourself. Those things depend on your
own spiritual sensitivity, otherwise you would not feel it
that strongly.   Spiritual sensitivity is proportional to the
growth of your spiritual energy.

*Q: It was strong movement, different from the feeling of
bliss. It seemed to come from inside me, but perhaps not.*

Master Ni: At the beginning your channel was not open, so
it was experienced as strong movement.   Once the other
channels are all open, it will not be a strong feeling.

Also, there is knowledge about half-achieved spiritual
beings who wish to steal energy from a woman or a man.
Sometimes that happens and needs to be guarded against
by your spiritual practice.

I think your main question is about the soul. As I have
said, everything is Tao, so I would like to give examples
from daily life to show how we can best cultivate ourselves;
specifically, how to channel personal or group spiritual
energy.

In a natural ancient society, where no dominant organized religion has been practiced, natural spiritual phenomenon can be easily observed.   The vast country of
China has many different regions.   Some people are educated and some are not, but, either way, different customs

and worship have been passed down from one generation to the next. At the time I was in China, no plumbing system existed, so we obtained our water from wells. A well is dug at the site of a spring, and usually stones are placed around the mouth to make the rim stable. Because of the care that is taken to make the well, and because it supports such an important part of life, people have pleasant feelings and respect for the well. Women in the village who experience some frustration in their life or in their marriage relationship, from the suffering of poverty or disharmony with in-laws, may go to the well for help. It is a well-known practice that some ordinary women pray to the well. They believe that because the spring below is inexhaustible, a goddess must be located there. The power of visualization or belief would usually bring a positive result for a woman who prays to the well.

Also, when I was young and living in China, most of the trees in my community were cut down to create farm land to provide food for the population. Occasionally you would see a banyan, a big tree several hundred years old, still standing. Under this tree would be a small altar where people worshipped. The people were worshipping the place where the tree god helped the banyan survive for so long. They believe the tree must possess a special power, so they prayed there and made offerings. For example, if a woman is newly married, and if she is not pregnant after the first year, her husband's family will worry, because children who become young farm hands are important to the rural lifestyle. If she is still not pregnant by the second year, this becomes a big concern. By the third year, she has disappointed the family. So some women pray to the trees in the countryside and they become pregnant. This is one way for people to channel their spiritual energy. They get a response because their chosen image, the tree or the well, is their connection to the divine. They also get a response because of the simplicity of their lives, their sincerity and their goodness.

Some places in rural areas have a strange but beautiful piece of stone. Some of these stones are carved in the shape of a human being, not highly artistic work, just ordinary craftsmanship. People worship or beg blessings from these stones and get a response. This is not a joke, it is a serious practice for many people. In ancient times, there were no public toilets, no toilets at all. Men could urinate anywhere, but they were afraid to do so on these stones; they had respect for them.

When I was growing up in China, we used an earthen, wood-burning stove for cooking. When you have food to cook on it, the stove is a special and important place in a household. The family gathers around the stove to eat the nutritious food. Because of its importance and its benefit to the life of the family, many people think a divinity is present that can help the family prosper, so they worship their earthen stove. These people pray to the stove for prosperity or blessing. They get a response and because of their constant efforts, it becomes an important spiritual practice for them.

As another example, a beautiful statue of a young girl, Miss Beauty, is revered by teen-age girls. Girls who have acne on their faces, go to her and pray, "Help cleanse my face. I will offer up the modern cosmetic powders and creams in return." So on the altar of this so-called Miss Beauty, many cosmetics are given as thankful offerings.

You may think this is strange, but people in some places worship snakes and rats, thinking they can bring prosperity, power or position. Some people worship monkeys; and are afraid of the monkey spirits. People who live in the foothill villages think it is the monkey spirits that make problems for their children. They worship the monkeys to bring peace and protection to their youngsters.

A less attractive form of worship is practiced by some minority tribes in the backward regions of China. On the fifth day of the fifth lunar month, they put many kinds of insects and animals such as spiders, scorpions, snakes, frogs and so forth, in a big jar or wooden box. After 49 days, they take out the survivor. They worship this survivor and take this practice seriously. Also, every three years they poison a person to make a sacrifice to a special insect god. This is done from their wish for protection. That is not a healthy way to channel spiritual energy.

Sophisticated city people who have a little religion sometimes dedicate a temple. In this temple, they put beautiful statues, some with robes as rich and elegant as those of ancient royalty. Some of the robes are decorated with gold. The people think these images can help them and, practically, that is one way to channel spiritual energy. You might call it idol worship, but it works; a response occurs, otherwise no one would do it.

There is another kind of animal worship that I feel I cannot escape telling you about. In northern China, the villagers worship the fox and the weasel, which is a rodent that looks like a large yellow rat and can kill chickens. The weasel is bigger than a rat but smaller than a cat, a fierce animal. They worship that. They are afraid of it. They do not like people to talk about foxes or weasels, and they refer to those animals as "the fox fairy" and "the great yellow fairy." You see, smart animals can trick humans.

Sometimes the people erect images of spiritual deities to worship as the guardians of the village. In a certain festival, people of two villages will meet. Depending on whether the relationship between their villages is amiable or not, the festival may turn out to be a war of gods or goddesses, although the original purpose of the festival was peace and friendliness.

From observing all these things, one might surmise that the high religions like Christianity or Islam just pray to the air as some Chinese farmers pray to trees. It is the same thing. Moses, for example, saw the bush aglow. Then the bush started talking; it was his personal, sole experience. Objectively, humans have spiritual energy. This spiritual energy needs to be wisely channelled. It is like having electricity but not conducting it through a wire. In humans the spiritual energy is much more subtle than electricity. Taoists have a way to channel this spiritual energy. So the development of Taoism is a history of the collection of the many ways to channel your spiritual energy for it best and most effective use. Those practices are usually considered secret.

In ancient times, people also occasionally used spiritual power to manipulate society or other people. In our tradition, learning spiritual power is extremely serious. For example, training a student in martial arts is a virtuous discipline. You have to have virtue, be kind, and have understanding and sympathy. Only after the teachers discover you are trustworthy do they give you those techniques. Primarily, all practice directs you to respect everything and, thus, to embrace the respectful orientation within your own life-being. It is another way to channel your spiritual energy. Religions usually set up statues or images and through certain ritual practices, one's spiritual energy is channeled. Nature and the spiritual world may respond to you, leaving you to wonder if something was accomplished through your own spiritual energy or not.

The most significant way to channel your spiritual energy is when every statue means something and every ritual means something. Most important is the essence: your quiet respectful mood within and controlling your spiritual nature with good concentration.

My point is this: many religious people have beneficial experiences because there is a response to channeling one's energy before an image. Therefore, they learn that spiritual existence is real. But because they limit themselves to one religious system, they think theirs is the only way. The result is that they squabble with people of other religious beliefs. That is a setback and shows the undevelopment of human spiritual consciousness in the social world.

Christian seminaries, Catholic schools or other religious schools always teach a subject called comparative religion but, in reality, they do not see the internal part of it. Students learn only the structures of the concepts and theories, things that are not spiritually important at all. The most important thing is: do you have sincerity within? There is an ancient Chinese proverb that says, "If you have sincerity within, mountains can be moved and oceans can be filled." If you do not have sincerity, a matter as simple as picking a branch from a tree cannot be done. So sincerity, spiritual sincerity itself, is the most powerful thing.

Earlier, we observed that any object a person believes to be holy can cause a response. Praying to stars, the sun and the moon has all doubtlessly been employed by ancient people. For myself, I think the sky is a more fitting object of worship than some temporal establishment, or a personal creation. It extends so far and wide, nobody can appropriate the whole sky system as a creation belonging only to a certain group. It is a natural creation. However, behind the sky is the subtle truth and the subtle law and that is what a student of Tao, a student of ultimate truth, follows. We do not follow shining stars, we follow a deeper reality.

I would also like to mention that in most ordinary circumstances, people who project their minds clearly and strongly can cause things to happen, even without any spiritual or religious formality. One person described to me that his wife was looking for a certain kind of car but had only a little money and a small amount of time to search. Just single-mindedly looking, holding that kind of image in her mind, she immediately found the right thing, exactly what she was looking for. You can consider that a projection of spiritual energy caused the response.

Many stockbrokers can pick a nicely performing stock to make money. A stockbroker might do well for other people, because he does it out of spiritual energy, but when he does it for his own account, he experiences a lot of concern which disturbs the spiritual energy so he does not do as well as he did for others.

Consider when a man is attracted to a woman and a woman is attracted to a man. For example, you are a young man and you meet a certain girl. If you find her interesting, you are subtly telling her, "Hey, this girl is interesting." It is just your psychological response. The girl, even with no verbal communication, will immediately know that and respond to it. We do not need to go deeply into this, but this example gives you another indication of the power of spiritual energy.

When my tradition trains students, the first discipline is not to encourage them to have all kinds of ambition, to project their power onto the small matters of life, but only to gather their power for doing the important practices concerning spiritual health and immortality. However, the subtle projection between a man and a woman without any prayer gives evidence of the subtle projection causing a response without the use of a formal object of worship.

Several things are highly recommended to any person who wishes to channel spiritual power to bring benefit to the world and then to seek high spiritual achievement. First, you need to recognize the law of natural response. The natural world is not inert, it responds to sincere requests. You, for your part, have spiritual energy. Second, the practice you do channels your spiritual energy and cause a corresponding response of natural energy. The content of that response will be determined by the kind of practice that is being done. Third, the subtle, clear thoughts that you project are more effective than your confused thoughts. A spiritual student always needs to eliminate scattered thoughts, then the projection will be strong and useful.

This is all to teach you to watch your thoughts. Many people who have upsetting lives need only to look at their personal thoughts to see how they invite trouble and cause unfortunate happenings. A chapter in *The Way of Integral Life* describes how small thoughts in your mind can sound louder than thunder. Always watch the small thoughts. You may believe that people, the world and nature do not know what you are thinking, but your thoughts always can be known, because you are in a sphere of energy composition which projects your energy according to the way you manage your life energy.

We each have a substantial responsibility to channel our internal personal destiny, our personal life and our personal spiritual being, though our awareness of this may vary. It is important. Surely I am not saying you can totally manage whatever happens to you; that is overambitious in the sphere of fleshly life. Although in some ways we can moderate the happenings in our lives, we still have a natural, inborn destiny in the background, In some way you set a special pattern. Each person is a pattern in which certain things happen easily; certain kinds of luck come easier to some of us than to others. We need to understand that the energy arrangement is a destiny and recognize what we need to overcome and how much we can do by ourselves. We cannot be overambitious.

I would like to give you an example of different levels. One person, Chang, before he was my student, was adopted by a woman. Her father was a Taoist. She was a spiritual leader in a small community and she was going to die. Because she was a generous person who was doing well financially, she gave alms and help to all kinds of people. Her son had a friend, Mo, from a minority tribe, Meo, who were a little more primitive than the Han people. Sorry to mention that, but the people of the minority tribe had more spiritual power than the ordinary Han people who were more intellectual. This tribe had more spiritual practice and its members were more single-minded. So the woman and her son invited the friend's help to see if she could be cured. He agreed to help and he wrote down a formula which included some herbs and a bird. The bird that was needed was an owl. Owls appear only at night, so one night the son and his friend went to a tree. By contacting the spiritual tree, the friend Mo made the bird fall to the ground, and they were able to bring home a live owl.

The friend had the power to do this. So with the bird and herbs he made a concoction for the woman, but the woman's life was not saved, and she passed over. This story relates to the truth that human life and death are different magic.

When you talk about increasing longevity or something similar, you might be able to do something about it, providing that you, yourself, work to be achieved through the right practice. Although other people may be able to help, there is a natural limitation over all people and all life beings. For example, Jesus' fortune was different from that of Moses, Mohammed, Sakyamuni, Confucius and Lao Tzu. All fortunes are different. If we come to the stage where we pick up a human shape, then we have that natural limitation.

We are like trees; there are small trees and big trees. There are grasses of different size. If you talk about differences, you can even find differences on the leaves on the same tree. Each leaf is unique. So destiny is not common, it is not the same in general. I would like to discuss at another time how we can best handle and work with our personal destiny.

Do not be prejudiced or superstitious, but learn something from ancient spiritual education to help you channel your own spirit. I recommend utilizing an image of one you respect, like a statue of Quan Yin, the picture of Master Lu, your teacher or yourself, to channel your energy through constructive visualization.

Most people know and say, "the body is the temple of your god," but so few people respect the temple. Mostly they disrespect, abuse and mistreat the temple, and at the same time they also mistreat and abuse their god. They acquire external decorations of spirituality without knowing how to relate spiritual accomplishment to their own life-beings to bring about a good, healthy, constructive life.

IX
Sincerity is the Power of God
(The Root of All Spiritual Power)

My tradition does not encourage students to be spiritually prejudiced or superstitious, like other religions that take advantage of people's superstitions in order to control them. We wish that people would channel their spiritual energy by living quietly and respectfully all the time. This means they need to have spiritual sincerity. The root of all spiritual power is sincerity. Even without religious practice, with just that single spiritual energy, you can achieve what you aim at. If you choose something tangible, you may end up like Paul Getty and Howard Hughes, two famous rich people in the world. I do not think they worshipped the god of money or the god of wealth. They created themselves as people of wealth through their sincere dedication to the making of money. I am not encouraging you to do that. What you do is your own choice. But there are much higher and more lasting things for you to invest your energy in, rather than what can be summed up by numbers or played with for only a short time.

Sincerity is spiritual achievement and that is our direction. The practice is to channel your spiritual sincerity. Then you can achieve what needs to be done with gentleness and subtlety, accomplishing more than people who use violence, loud voices and noise. These people create turmoil. Also, spiritual students should especially not neglect the fact that many beneficial material inventions and new theories were discovered with the help of individual spiritual energy. Without it, great breakthroughs could not have been brought about. Edison, Einstein, Planck and many other people who used their achievements to improve our lives did it with spiritual energy. Conversely, many people who consider themselves religious may use the name of religion to create trouble. Such people are negative and sick, not like people living a normal life, not like people facing the broad direction of life.

It is interesting to see that in the west, it is the general convention or belief that spiritually, God has multiple functions. Whatever troubles people have, they go to the same God. For example, if they need money, then God is the god of money. If they wish to have children, it is God that helps reproduction. So when people are in trouble God is a great helper. It is just one name, God, that is addressed to accomplish many functions and each person uses it a little differently. In the west, at the dinner table, each person has different spoons, different forks and different knives, each one for a different purpose. It is the opposite in China: at the dinner table, a pair of chopsticks and a spoon serve all the purposes. It is so simple. In eating, the Chinese way is simple. In religion, the western way is simple. In worshipping, Chinese folks are more complicated. They have all kinds of gods that do different things. The Christian God is like the chopsticks on the Chinese dinner table, and the Chinese gods are like the set of forks and knives and spoons on the American dinner table.

My main point is that, according to the law of spiritual response, how you project your mind determines what will echo back positively as spiritual or psychological help during your stages of growth.

Now I would like to talk about the names of spirits. All spirits are natural. Once people become enamored of honored titles, they immediately addressed spirits in the same way. It was out of ignorance that people have not known how to address the spirits. In the countryside of China, people worship the big trees. They name a large tree "Great General." Some people worship snakes and designate the snake as "Great King." Out of psychological need, in local temples, people worship different statues with different titles.

Chinese villagers have come to worship many gods in the last 1,500 years since the government promoted religion as an adjunct to political rule. If we consider them objectively, we see that there are two types of titles given to spiritual images. One type is the family relation type. In China, people use the titles, "father of heaven," or "grandfather of heaven." The ocean fishermen call the goddess of the ocean "grandma of the ocean." Similarly, endearing titles are used to name the spirits. In northwestern China, a large population of Chinese, the Hu tribes, adopted Islam. Islamic people title God as Allah, but the Hu tribe calls God the "big brother of Hu." You see, spirits have no titles, but humans, out of affection or just because they need a powerful support, call spirits or spiritual images as father, mother, brother or sister. This is one way.

Another way is to call them kings, queens, princes or princesses. When that manner of address began, the world had already changed. In the political conception, kings, queens and other royalty presented themselves as lords. Because the spiritual world was seen as the ruler, such names were used. This has been done since ancient times, but it is highly misleading, reflecting only a projection of human behavior on the spiritual world. Since the center of society usually has kings, queens, princes or princesses who manifest the power of ruling, by using these names the common people receive an unhealthy, incorrect concept about natural spirits. This becomes a setback to their spiritual growth, because they do not learn spiritual reality. While convenient as titles, these names affect people psychologically, making them unable to know clearly the reality of the spirits. Religions or religious activities that use family relationships, social titles or political designations unintentionally represent the spiritual world as volatile, making people lock into one side of the human world without leading them deeply into the spiritual world.

My point here is that all spirit is natural. There are no rulers in the spiritual world; everything is natural, differentiated only by energy. Spirits respond to people without gender discrimination. A natural spirit can be addressed as mother or father and need not have any blood relationship with you at all. They are natural spirits. Therefore, as you use certain practices to develop yourself a little more, you will see the truth of the spiritual world. This will help those who have intellectual capacity to also develop spiritual ability. Such a person will only trust what is true and make the truth a guide and path for daily life. In this way, no confusion or misconception will be fostered about the spiritual world. This is a responsibility for the new generation which is looking for spiritual development, and it is even more important for a spiritual student.

The name "God" is often used as another name for human ego to some people. Those egotistical people find expression in preaching the doctrine of the dominance of God. What were good words at the beginning have slowly come to be the expression of stubborn ego in today's use. It is not all people who are that way, fortunately.

In the spiritual world, ego is something that derives from the lower animal nature. Slowly, the function of ego was formed. God is not in the domain of ego. Although in human language we have not yet found a better word for God, the teaching of Tao expresses the wholeness of divinity. For example, we already have some idea of the law of spiritual response: the response is not from one side, but comes from both sides. Business orientation finds a business response. Sexual orientation causes a response on the sexual level. A spiritually centered orientation causes a response from the spiritual level. It is the same principle of response, but the response matches the level at which you transmit or project. On the lower levels there is more ego involved. On the moral level, the pure spiritual level, there is no ego.

Religious practices are most often only another form of bargaining. "I trust you, I believe in you, I worship you, you protect me, you bless me, you comfort me. You are my god, you are my insurance company. You must cover me when I pay the premium." In that case, the person is established as the customer and God as the shop owner. It is a business connection, it is an ego practice. An achieved spiritual student can see through it. Are we extending our independence or are we extending personal ego?

When you feel the need of a religion, immediately check to see the benefit you wish to gain from your spiritual beliefs: confidence or spiritual learning. If the learning is to increase your pure spiritual development, it helps; then it is not the same as a belief system. A belief system consists of the believer and the believed; a bargain is struck and there is no independent justice. Justice turns out to be the success of the bargain. The presence of a bargain indicates the dualistic practice of self-splitting. A dualistic practice is like looking in a mirror and mistaking the image and your self to be different things. In this way, you keep bargaining with yourself.

X
The Spiritual Integral Truth

This is a warning. High spiritual achievement has no God. This does not mean there is no God. It means there is no ego; it means there is no dualistic practice. At that point, you reach the spiritual integral truth. Achieved spiritual students who have learned different practices will have senses so subtle that they are sensitive to different levels of spirit. In most ordinary spiritual practice, what part or side do you call God? What side of the mirror do you call self? Or is there another spirit who responds to you?

The spiritual truth is integral. It cannot be separated from the sincere unity of the image and the projector of the image. It is just this oneness.

Some people think I render a beneficial service in practicing Chinese medicine and some think I do a good job teaching different subjects of the precious Taoist heritage. Some find me helpful in the Chinese way of reading birth charts. Some find that I can teach chi gong and Tai Chi Ch'uan very well, and so forth. However, when I do these things for them, what is me? You cannot pick one location, or part or cell within me and call it the source of competent work. You cannot pull one hair from my arm and call that Master Ni. I can function because I am whole, not a collection of parts. The universe is a whole, not parts. You cannot cut out a certain part and call it holy, as most religious practices do. They set up a temple or church or a platform, then title and limit that part as holy. They do not see the whole thing. The practice of inside to outside depends on the moment that your level of projection reaches the level of response. The corresponding response depends on your level; it totally hinges on the level of energy. In our daily life, we are coarse, inconsiderate, egotistical or selfish, and in being so, we cut or disconnect pieces from the whole.

Somebody said that each individual is a small temple, a small office of God. Someone else said we are like small computers that hook up to a big, master computer. There must be a master computer, but how can you call your computer holier or less holy? There must be one master computer big enough to network all communication, to connect with all computers. If the connection between the master computer and the small ones were cut off, the master computer would no longer be the master. It would be an empty or dead computer, and be of no use. Do you call only the master computer holy? Do you not think the small computer is equal in importance?

Whatever your purpose is for utilizing the image of God or the belief in God, the level of motivation can be seen by what you are doing; that will determine whether your use is holy or unholy. People only relate to externals when they lose their balance and need something to rely on for emotional security. Or they just call on the divine for friendly emotional energy to support them in their failures, frustration, mistakes or disappointment. An improvement is needed, but not from that side; the improvement must take place on your side. It is not the images that need improving. The side that needs improving is yours. You must improve yourself, then the high God, the true God, will be with you. If you do not improve, you will travel around and around in your own circular patterns of behavior, locked into a closed system. That way is like continually feeding yourself junk. It is a process of self-poisoning.

Even if people have the same faith, each will use it differently. Each religion teaches the value of finding psychological consolation, a way to feel reassured in the face of incompletion, of personal spiritual shortcomings. Consolation or self-poisoning, it is all ego practice, not spiritual practice. Unless you know to jump out of such a psychological trap and get rid of the swollen-ego sickness, you may not see the light of Truth of true heaven. I do not know what other language you can use. Only after you are finished with the psychological pattern of trapping yourself in your ego will you allow yourself to see the light of true heaven. Simply, be earnest and know Tao.

Many people ask me, what is Tao? Is it not clear enough? Tao is integral truth. It is not a projection of a prejudice; it is not a partial truth that needs insistence; it is not a viewpoint or a philosophy. It is the universal integral truth, the truth of all lives, the truth that exists prior to any thought or statement. You may not be familiar with the terminology, but it does not matter. A name for the truth, a language for the reality, a picture of a person, a title of the spirit, helps some, but it is not real. It is just as you make it, but the program is really your limitation. Names, titles, special vocabularies, pictures or images may help some people's lives but they are still not spiritual reality. They are what people make of them. All such established religious programs are ultimately limitations. Once you break away from these poor psychological skills you are attached to, the openness and broadness lets you become spiritually all-reachable, all-approachable. If you are all-reachable or all-approachable spiritually, you embrace the entire spiritual world and the entire spiritual world embraces you. There is no separation.

Integral truth is not a uniting of all religions; it is doing away with all religions. Use your mind to directly reach the universal mind. Use your spirit to directly reach the universal spirit. Surely in human life, religion is a matter of different customs in different societies. Achieved ones never disagree with customs and also never agree with any custom. They live, they are happy and they may enjoy the customs, but their spiritual development is never limited or confined by them. An integral person is a directly achieved person of integral truth. This person embraces integral truth without conflicting with or becoming prejudiced by the customs of the society in which he or she was raised.

Subscribing to most religions is like getting on a bus that promises to take the undeveloped souls to a different camp. But it turns out to be a concentration camp. You need to choose a spot to get off, otherwise the end of the ride is where you end your life. It is better to choose spiritual education which makes you wise and able to manage your life.

Learn the universal spiritual education of Tao which helps you attain spiritual independence. Spiritually, you are self-responsible. Spiritually, you do not need another ruler or authority to set you in good order or to straighten out your life. This you can do yourself by learning from the universal spiritual education of Tao.

Please read *The Story of Two Kingdoms* for a further discussion of these and related topics.

CONCLUSION:
TO ACHIEVE THE INNER LIGHT

In ancient times, people were inspired by nature to develop themselves. Because the cycles of nature claimed their attention, so they were inspired to discover the force that drove the universe. Who or what was turning the big cyclic wheel of nature and causing seasonal changes? Obviously, when they gazed at the stars, they discovered that the stars also moved. After observing the stars for a period of time, they noticed that the Big Dipper does not travel from horizon to horizon like the other stars, but turns around and around with the North Star at its center.

In this way they came to believe that the Big Dipper was the hub of a great wheel. The other stars that traveled across the sky could be grouped into 28 constellations; the part of the wheel that turned the most, from horizon to horizon, they divided into twelve sections; these are known as the twelve houses of the zodiac. In English this is referred to as the twelve signs of the zodiac, not the twelve houses.

After many generations of observing the stars and other natural phenomena, their wondering minds expanded to look for knowledge beyond the small scope of their own existence. This knowledge was the foundation on which they established a faithful relationship with nature. They discovered that there was a constancy in the changes of nature; that spring always followed winter, etc. This is how the ancient people were naturally inspired to develop religious faith.

The appearance of religious faith occurred not only among ancient people of the Chinese region near the Yellow River, but also among the ancients on the Nile in Egypt and the Euphrates in Babylonia (now Iraq). Traces of primitive religious faith have also been found along the Ganges River in India. Such natural religious expressions demonstrate the first attempts of the ancients to enlarge their scope of knowledge. Their interest had evolved from merely dealing with material things to an awareness of the heavens. It was a type of communication of our human ancestors with the sky.

More valuable than watching how the stars moved was their deep feeling of connection with the sky. This natural type of religion was not organized at the beginning; it may have been somebody's natural inspiration or a response to a deep feeling of relationship with nature. This type of occurrence is a spontaneous happening, because all people are very deeply connected with nature.

This natural, personal expression is totally different from what most people experience today, now that so many people are city dwellers, living in controlled environments. They do not directly experience or realize their deep connection with the cycles of nature; the deep feeling is there, but they do not recognize it or know its source. Therefore, one of four things can happen: 1) they move to the country, 2) they read books to learn about it, 3) somebody with a developed mind comes along and teaches them to transfer their feeling to a social movement or other activity - this can be either positive or negative - or 4) they misguide themselves or are misguided into behavior that is destructive towards themselves or others. If you are interested, you can study how human society was managed by strong leaders and investigate the main ways in which people can be controlled: by means of religion, military power and politics. These three institutions divert a person's attention away from nature. As a result, people lose their relationship with nature. These controlling systems usurp people's natural faith for their own exploitative purposes. Anybody who has power over anyone else, no matter what the form, can manipulate the other. I am, of course, making a generalization; there are always a few individuals in any profession who sincerely work to help others. Those few, however, cannot exert much influence.

If and when individuals perceive that military and political control do not answer the deepest needs in their lives, some look to religion and others go further and look for the spiritual truth. Those who look to religion only, probably focus on a set of general religious beliefs, which is, in essence, an unquestioned accumulation of customs. They learn the customs, not the truth. The people who understand the limitations of organized religion keep looking for something else. I call those people "students of spiritual truth." Such a person wants to learn what brought the customs about originally. He distances himself from the influence of the social institution of religion, but not from its most important practices. He wants to learn the truth or the meaning behind what was originally practiced when the custom arose and how to employ these truths for his own well being and for the well being of the world. We are not making any emotional complaint about social religions being bad; rather, we are seriously seeking truth in the original material. We wish to know how it will benefit us; that is more important than belonging to a religious club.   Let's not be confused by emotional creations, social coercion or peer pressure. Such forces make religion an escape from the reality of the difficulty of life. We know that when a person escapes the difficulty of his life, he stays on the shallow surface or superficial level of life. Escaping reality causes him to lose his deep connection with the natural joy or bliss of life that comes with being human.

We need to learn how the natural sphere deeply relates with human spirits. What is the evidence that there are spirits? What is the truth about them? Later generations of religious teachers who were without the natural inspiration of the spiritual world did not teach in a healthy manner. Even if what they teach contains elements of truth, it is being used, either consciously or unconsciously, to control students.

Through my own spiritual development and through over 2 million years of the spiritual development of the ancestors of the heritage of Tao, it has been discovered that the souls of humans are strongly related to and connected with the sun. Today, people conceive of God in the image of an external sovereign who rules over nature, kings and leaders, and all people. But this is the conception of people who do not yet know truth; they have had no experience of it. Practically, if a person directly reaches the deep truth of spirituality, he or she will know that the God-impulse is coming from the sun. Similarly, if a person directly receives inspiration from nature, his idea or image of God will be similar to his experience of the sun, the moon and the stars, and will finally come back to the sun. Let us take, as an illustration, the Egyptians. If we go past the general level of cultural customs, and if we take away the colorful garments of religion, such as the gold ornaments adorning King Tut's tomb, we will find that the spiritual Egyptian people worshipped the sun. Again, if we deeply study the history and religion of the Babylonian people, we will find at the root that they worshipped the sun. If we continue to study ancient practices in other parts of the world, we will discover that the original Indian spiritual practitioners and the Aztecs also worshipped the sun. Surely, the sun is God. Let us think about what we consider as Godly qualities and see if they apply here. The sun is impartial. It gives light, life and warmth to everybody, equally, without discrimination. There are many other Godly qualities, such as reliability, beneficence and creativity.

Some of the human minds of later generations who knew the truth did not want to reveal their knowledge. They knew that the naturalness of life becomes an obstruction to any ruling system, so they led people to believe in an abstract, artificial God. Those who understood the truth that God is the sun, and did not wish to support artificial situations, retreated from worldly life to live quietly. We call them natural Taoists or people of the natural essence.

Practically, we receive the gift of our lives from the sun. We are spiritually still deeply related with the sun. Ancient people studied nature and realized that the sun is connected with the human natural vitality. The bright sunshine represents the yang energy, the impetus of all natural lives.

Human life also has a mind. Just as the moon in the sky reflects the sun's light, the human mind reflects human life. The human mind is the reflection that comes about when a person who is trying to be good in life discovers that no matter how well-intentioned he may be, he still somehow, in a way he cannot explain, constantly makes trouble. This internal reflection induces the development of the mind.

Ancient people studied nature and therefore realized that lunar energy is connected with the development of our intelligence of mind. A bright full moon represents the full intelligence of an individual. That brightness represents the clarity, purity and fullness which the mind wishes to achieve.

So the sun is the source of all life, and the moon is the symbol of the development of the mind. How about the stars? On other occasions, I have revealed secrets about the body.

I have written how a healthy human body is a company of many spirits. Not only is there a soul and a mind, there are also spirits. I also gave a description of how you develop yourself to experience the existence of these spirits. This spiritual practice is the soul party and is described in my book *Quest of Soul.* From the evidence and proof given by the ancestors of our tradition, we truly believe the spirits and the internal spiritual vitality we receive are from the stars. Those spirits are like a small strand of gentle silk. They live everywhere inside a person's body, just as the stars are scattered all across the night sky.

In the sky, we see that the Big Dipper is the center of this part of the universe, because all the other stars turn around it. So the seven stars of the Big Dipper (or nine if the North Star and the one star which is a double star are included), when combined, represent or are the authority over the spirits. A diagram of the Big Dipper is seen in the beginning of the work, *The Book of Changes and the Unchanging Truth.*

In the ancient spiritual approach, the sun meditation and sun practice, moon meditation and moon practice were natural parts of the spontaneous spiritual expression, but after the culture developed more, people began to paint over the natural background of human spiritual reality. After many layers of paint, people lost the true vision of the real source and connection to human life and spiritual faith. They lost the knowledge that people are born into a flesh body and are also equipped with a soul, mind and spirits.

The interesting, valuable practices still exist, but because later people are dependant on cultural creations, they miss the truth. For example, ancient people all worshipped the stars, but later religions referred to them as gods, deities, buddhas or boddhisatvas. For example, an important sect of Buddhism reveres the Buddha called Amitabha. Buddha means sage. Amitabha was originally another name for Venus, the morning and evening star, which enlightened Sakyamuni as he meditated under the Bodhi Tree.

Whether you go to Tibet, Rome, India or China, the ancient spiritual buildings all have paintings of the heavenly bodies. You will also find them in the Greek legends such as the Odyssey. You can find them in the Christian tradition, also as with the Star of Bethlehem, but somewhat less prominently because that tradition is quite removed from its sources, most directly, Judaism. Islam is also based on Judaism. The Judaic background is a collection of Egyptian and Babylonian experience and basically, Egypt and Babylonia had the religion of stars. It was from this religious worship of the sky that astrology developed. Basically the background of all the religious traditions originates in the stars; there is no further secret here beyond that.

Student: When I was in France, I visited one of the old citadels with walls around it and towers and so forth. We went into the ancient church there. I believe it was a Christian church. The inside was decorated differently than the churches here. The ceiling was painted dark blue and stars were painted all over it. It was beautiful.

Master Ni: It is beautiful. There are no boundaries or differences among religions that can really be maintained because, practically, all ancient religions worshipped the same thing: the sky. But later people used their minds to paint things over differently, so one group could think its star is brighter than the others.

My main point is that the different religions, aside from any accurate psychological applications, are just of the sky. No one needs to go into a church or temple to know about the sky or to relate oneself spiritually with it. The sky belongs to everybody. There is no conflict that can be based upon the sky, spiritually or physically.

So if we would like to make progress in looking for the truth, we need first to tear down the old fences of religious differences. I mentioned that the soul practice, or sun practice, benefits your soul. Anybody can learn it, why make a religion out of it? It is from the old Taoist tradition, and it is given as a practice. The moon meditation benefits the mind. If done correctly, your mind is much clearer. If you do not do it right, however, the mind becomes twisted and you will suffer. What we call the Hun and Po are also connected with the sky. The Hun, the high spirits, comes from the sun and returns to the sun. The Po, the physical spirits, are connected with the moon and stars. The two are clearly very different types of natural energy.

We are children of nature, or of the universe, and we are small models of nature. Because we are exactly as nature, the internal and external can respond to each other.

As I mentioned before, there are two kinds of people looking for truth. One kind looks for a group to join, because he likes the feeling of connecting with a big society. For him, it is sort of like a relationship with a friend or is a type of imaginary security he can hold onto. He does not necessarily learn anything useful, but he has a good time there.

The other is a spiritual student looking for realistic progress. Natural spiritual practices benefit your soul, mind and spirits. They do not expend your life-energy in order to become somebody else's spiritual slave or cattle. You learn from your teacher to develop yourself. That is important.

This book has the words *Inner Light* in its title. From where comes the Inner Light? It is the real connection with the true spiritual source. With the knowledge of the true source, everyone can reach the inner light. Because we are blocked by our own, or somebody else's, conceptual creations, we cannot see the truth. Truthfully, the commandments, tenets, dharmas and doctrines are only toys. They are given to us just as a toy is given to a baby in a cradle, to keep it from crying. Please go beyond even the doctrines I give you. Find out inside yourself what is the truth. Those toys can stop people from crying for a while, but they do not really help our growth. A baby's growth depends on its own internal vitality, never on a plastic toy purchased in a store.

In my teaching, I do not sell plastic toys; I just say, let's grow together so we can avoid the constant trouble generated in this world by insistence and stubbornness of different conceptual creations. In some ways, we have not developed anything real beyond the first discovery that the sky is connected with our life. Our cultural developments and achievements are self-deceptive because they are too far away from the initial reality. Naturalness does not need decoration.

Fortunately, the new scientific approach is a little closer to the realistic sphere of nature than the religious emotions of some of our human ancestors. However, it only concerns itself with energy on the surface; it does not go deeply enough, which makes it impossible for people to be balanced. It takes more than one side to have something be complete, just as hands must work together and both sides of the brain must help each other. Communism, for example, is the mischievous child of the philosophy of materialism. It has taken over China. But despite the fact that Communism has been in power for forty years, the practice or performance of Chi Gong is coming back actively. The reality of the spiritual side of life cannot be abolished by political rules or regulations. The government does not allow members of the Communist party to be religious believers, so they have changed the name of healing activities to Chi Gong. Chi Gong means "breathing practice," but in reality, it is mostly spiritual healing when you go into it deeply. Even chi itself is semi-physical and semi-spiritual, and cannot be totally materialized. Authorities must admit its existence because it works, as with the healing modality of acupuncture.

I would like to give you some examples that are happening with Chi gong in China today. There are two famous chi gong practitioners or healers. One is a young doctor named Neing Shing, who is a traditional Chinese doctor in addition to knowing Western medicine, and who has many special powers. When he is presented with a case he cannot handle by writing a Chinese herbal prescription or by applying his own power to it, he will write a prescription called a "chi gong prescription." Practically, he does not reveal the truth to the world that a spiritual being is doing the job of providing the prescription. He is a trained Chinese doctor, able to write prescriptions, but when he does not have the ability to perform some particularly difficult job, he needs to invite a spirit to enter his body to accomplish it. But he does not tell people about this; instead, he describes it as chi gong, a breathing exercise. I am saying the spirit comes into his body and writes a prescription for strong herbal medicine for the patient. Some of those herbs, if used incorrectly, would be poisonous, so all doctors avoid using them. He has to call it chi gong, however, because under the Communist system no one can safely say that there is a spirit that can live without physical manifestation; their dogma is that humans have no souls. But in reality, most Chinese know that is not the truth. If they do not know it, it is because the Communist education has twisted their understanding to fit the dogma of materialism.

Another type of Chi Gong practitioner has the power to make himself disappear. He also can take something from a tightly sealed bottle or from a house or anywhere. Once this person was making a special demonstration of his skill and discovered that his energy was not strong enough. There were many spiritual entities, spiritual powers, belonging to the level of vibration he could reach, so they came to help him accomplish his performance in front of many scientists. However, in a Communist country, nobody can talk about there being spirits present.

Although you cannot see them, there are many invisible lives right beside you. Once you reach them, they can help you because they are smarter and more capable. In China today, even the students in the medical classes cannot discuss the Hun and Po. There is no mention of it. They must treat them as material objects in the textbooks. Many have been persecuted and died under the Communist materialistic doctrine. However, a shallow materialistic doctrine can never be a substitute for true spiritual reality.

I like to share my doctrine. My doctrine is a doctrine of no doctrine. It does not mean "nothing," it is the learning of zero doctrine. What is more important is that I am expecting your development. If you, my dear friends, develop yourselves there is no problem. We will not feel separated. I will not need to worry about you making trouble for yourselves or somebody else.

Beloved friends, most of you were born into a conventional society where the convention is Christianity and Jesus is a god. When he was born into the world, what sign was present? The shepherds in the wilderness saw a bright star that had ascended, pointing the way to the inn where the young Christ lay. There were also three sages or saints, whom you call wise men, that came with gifts from the East. They followed the star, step by step searching for the god they knew was being born into the world. They finally found the inn and the baby in the manger. So they offered their gifts and blessed the baby.

Dear friends, it is from the stars that we know god. There are gods. They are connected with the stars. That is where the image came from. Gods also sometimes come from people, but we should not mentally cut off a god's connection with nature to create a separated entity. Gods of nature are not rulers of the human world nor are they judges of the human soul. They are just a different life form. I have a book in Chinese that would be interesting for all of you to read. It is hard to find a helper to translate it, because it is a gathering together of pieces compiled into a book about people during the stage of history around 5,000 years ago. During that time, many great leaders were born into the world from the stars, bringing with them starry energy.

I mentioned that the meditations of the sun, moon and stars were practiced by the ancient people. This practice means I can, myself, settle down my life with the simple essences of the sun, the moon and the stars, and do my simple practice of spiritual integration. The sun, moon and stars are illuminating sources of nature. Without them, can you imagine what kind of world this would be? Human life would not be able to make evolutionary progress in the dark. However, nature is original. As the Tai Chi diagram shows, there is an illumined source that lights up the dark world. It already existed long before the human race was born. Human people all have the necessary support for their lives from nature. The sun and moon existed before humans were born. People received the sun and moon as part of the nutrition in the natural womb. The sun does not change, the moon does not change and the stars do not change. But not much real progress has been made in human spirituality although the sun, moon and stars still shine upon us.

Until we grow our Inner Light, which sometimes I call the Subtle Light, a human being cannot really grow or mature spiritually. All ancient primitive people knew to do the sun practice, moon practice and star practice to remain with the primitive or basic spirituality of nature. But in the end, it does not bring the happiness, true peace or true growth that people look for. It is only a step on the way to change.

The Inner Light is something different from the inspiration of an artist. The Inner Light or Subtle Light is also something different from the ordinary wise person who obtains his wisdom through difficulties. The Inner Light is the spiritual energy of the universe. After years of cultivation, a person receives the Inner Light. Its power builds and increases when he uses his internal light to shine upon a matter. When he encounters trouble, he sees the way out of the problem or difficult matter.

Today, people do not only rely on the natural sources of light, they use electric lights or other kinds of artificial light. Those lights are all external. Yet with all this light, people still live in the dark. With the help of all external light, human happiness or the true joy of life does not increase. They live a life of constantly brewing confrontation and conflict within, and with other life beings. Joy does not increase until all people grow their Inner Light.

In ancient times, the sun, the moon or the Big Dipper were God to people. Those light sources present the opposite of confrontation, conflict and difficulty seen among people. They provided an image of a strong god that would govern nicely or help people. This is the ancient type of religion. Now as we see it, the worship of the sun, moon and stars has not satisfied people through these last 2,000 years. It is clearly to be seen that this type of worship is not the solution. Even when humans create religion as a support or governing power, it can be accepted in one place but make an enemy in another. So no one god or source of divinity can help the world or help human life. What is truly helpful is when each individual grows his own Inner Light to become the god of his own being. Then he can see what ought to be and what ought not to be; he can see what he should do and should not do.

This is my new spiritual direction for our new spiritual education. My work is not to promote a god to take care of all people; my new work is to educate all young gods and old gods to take care of themselves and to take care of their world, since no one god is strong enough to manage the entire human mind. So in my teaching, no specific god is exalted, recommended or promoted for any individual life, except the god of the Inner Light, your own Subtle Light. I have two important books specifically about this subject, which contain material gathered from my lectures. One is *The Uncharted Voyage Toward the Subtle Light*, and the other one is *The Footsteps of the Mystical Child.* My wish for you is that you can grow your Subtle Light. I wish that you will grow your Inner Light to be the god and savior of the world, your world.

You probably want to know how you can grow your own Inner Light. I repeat, you grow your own Inner Light when you find, by your own spiritual growth, your best solutions for the problems, situations, decisions or trouble in your life.

I am happy that all the gods and goddesses who are here in front of me treat me well, are open to me and accept me as a teacher, advisor and friend. I follow in the footsteps of my father. My father followed in the footsteps of our ancestors, offering spiritual service to our friends as an adjunct to our Chinese medical profession. Teaching is not our life source, thus, we do not hold a business attitude toward it, although we practice it seriously.

You know, on one level, all people are gods; but there are different types of god. Some transform their spiritual reality into money and power only, while other gods enjoy the openness of the opportunity of life. Just because there are different types of gods is no reason for discouragement or to shrink back from any healthy direction. What is important is what type of god we make ourselves to be. It is a spiritual choice. I follow in the footsteps of all my spiritual forefathers. That is the spiritual discipline I received and follow. We choose to be servers and guests, not competitors in the world.

World peace can be reached, but not through the struggle of establishing a powerful religion, or creating a powerful god who rules over all people. It cannot be done by suppressing all the other religions. Do you think that peace can be brought by causing conflict? The solution for the world is for each individual to grow his own Inner Light and see the spiritual reality in himself and in the world. This is the mission I choose; this is the work I do.

You do not need to learn the practice of the sun, moon and stars from me. It is ultimately important for people to enjoy nature. All ancestors did that already for a million years. People turn away from it and think of building their everlasting souls by making new chemical syntheses.

I am just a student of the ancient developed ones. I do not have the higher achievement. I have put together all my learning from them in different books as contributions of the sages. If you agree, each book can be a light source, an illuminator which can help kindle our inner light. A model center was set up in Atlanta by one of my students and friends, Frank Gibson, though all centers can operate independently or with a different structure. As for myself, although at present I am not doing any direct teaching, I will still give my time and energy to students who wish to be one of the spiritual illuminators, a source of light, among people. I teach for no charge because I wish for everyone to see the spiritual light. It is a dark world. Every individual needs sufficient Subtle Light within to shine upon his personal footsteps. To achieve that purpose, we need lots of intelligent, good-hearted people to share the same understanding about increasing our own spiritual awareness and putting aside our egos. Students can come study and see how centers can be set up. Also students may offer their help to work together to help each other learn through discussion and study.

I wish that there will be many spiritual illuminators who achieve themselves with the help of good teachers so that together we can work for today's world and tomorrow's peace, prosperity and health.

In ancient times, people projected their hopes onto another world and they called it the heavenly kingdom or pure land. With spiritual awareness, we would first fix the trouble, fix the darkness we received from the world. Then we can talk about the heavenly kingdom or pure land. All good teachers clearly know about it. All good teachers give their lives. They are not looking for personal longevity by keeping quiet to comply with the evil force. These people give up their own desire for a peaceful, quiet life and immortality to work for the benefit of others. They wish all people would wake up. They do not wish for a Heavenly reward; perhaps they did not even have any motive, intention or desire attached to their actions. They just gave their lives to be light, an example of spiritual self-development. They knew the world was in trouble and they wanted to show their fellows the way out.

The pure land is here. The heavenly kingdom is here. But there is no Buddha unless everybody is Buddha. There is no god unless everybody is god. When the competition for ego establishment ends, true peace will be seen.

Q: I grew up in a big and busy city and frequently visited the art museum there. In that museum, there are a great number of original paintings from the Christian tradition, mostly from the time of the Renaissance, I believe. It was always curious to me to see representations of Mary holding the baby Jesus. The baby would often be portrayed holding his hand up with the two first fingers upright and the other fingers folded. When I asked, they said that Jesus was giving a blessing. It was only after I began to read your books and learn a little chi gong practice that I made the connection that the hand position of the baby Jesus in the paintings is what you call the sword hand position. I am not yet sure about its use or meaning.

Master Ni: In ancient times, all people on earth worshipped the sun in a unified manner, although they lived far apart. The sun is God. Later, we described it differently, maybe because people's intellectual knowledge grew. Or perhaps there was no mention about the sun as God any more because the mind was strongly competing with the natural phenomenon. However, in lots of spiritual practices, you will discover that immortality connects with sun energy.

Aside from the conceptual religious creations, God to all earthlings was the sun. All ancient people worshipped the sun. They knew the source of life force. Their realistic spiritual practice connects with the three sources of the sun, moon and stars. Behind all the three is the subtle origin or Tao. The sun is the boss or king, the vital source of all lives. This I need to mention.

So if you dip deeply into all the religions, you can find that humans have one source. It is Tao, the subtle natural vitality. Even after the human ancestors scattered in different places, there was still the unified worship of the sun.

I obtained a piece of ancient writing. I would like to translate it here for you, but I do not necessarily hold it as the true reality of the beginning of the world. It may or may not be that way; it is an ancient record, not my writing. It is the way the people of the Chinese region viewed the development of the world; it is the law of natural development.

"All the things of the world come from the one. The one gives birth to three. All things are accomplished at five and become very prosperous at seven, then finally reach nine."

This declares that everything is in a process of development which can be divided into different stages. The numbers give the descriptions of the different stages and what positions they should be in. Therefore, because there are numbers involved, this also becomes a law of numbers. This knowledge comes from the ancient development of the universe. Now I need to carefully read this information to you. It reads as follows; I am not quoting directly.

The universe was undivided as one energy. It was indistinguishable. It was like an energy egg. Within the egg, the yoke was the center and the white surrounded it. Pang Gu was the one born within the egg. Pang Gu transformed himself nine times, during a short section of time. He still keeps changing. Before him, there was no inside and outside of the energy egg. It took a long time to transform the egg. The pure yang energy, the yolk, was continually developing to became heaven. The pure yin energy, the white, was continually developing to be the material sphere. Earth is one of the productions issuing from this process as the yin and the yang interplayed in the egg and stretched it out.

Pang Gu kept transforming himself. His growth set the height and the depth of the universe. The universe is his being. However, his spirit was supernature and had dominion over all the other creations in heaven and earth. The earth is also his body, the physical being of his life.

At the beginning of the earth, there were three big white birds that gave birth to all birds on earth. All life species were born much later than the appearance of those big birds.

Then, the first most powerful of creatures was born. This was the beginning of a world of all lives. The spirits did not yet know how to skillfully and effectively shape themselves.

So, the Heavenly authority, as the power symbol of all other creatures, had 13 heads. He would be our ancestor, although maybe we do not appreciate it, but that was the beginning of the work of self-making. We do not know whether we come from a bird with 13 heads, or we come from a snake with 9 heads, or through both of them. There were two ancient pictures to tell us how they looked.

Then, much later, a new species of people appeared, the authority of earth who became the power symbol of all creatures. Then, still much later, the new shape of people, seeing the authority of man who had nine heads was born. This time, the work of life shaping was better: 13 heads were reduced to 9. The brothers of authority of mankind all lived to a extremely old age. They divided the earth into nine regions separated by mountains and water. The nine brothers each took one region as a residence. Thereafter, different races and different developments occurred on each of the nine regions on earth. The process of human shape changed from huge to small, from clumsy to very adept.

Then, much later, but still long ago, people lived without houses. All people lived in caves. At that time, the size of life-forms become much smaller so that men could live in the caves, and they did not need to have so many heads, so they became much simplified; they were not like the rough nine-headed originals. During this stage, a wise leader found a way to shelter himself. He learned from the birds how to make a nest. This is how civilization started. This is how human society and the universe started according to the only existing record written on an earthen jar or plate. After that, a long period of time passed for which we have few records.

Ancient people were hermaphroditic; an individual had both male and female organs. An individual life itself was complete as a life being. This is something difficult for modern people to accept, so I would rather talk about the obscure Tao, because that makes you feel better. If I show you something too real, maybe because you did not experience it, you will reject it. I hope my talking about the hermaphroditic human did not make you misunderstand. It means that each individual was like a man and woman together, like the tai chi. That is why I draw lots of diagrams to represent that without giving the truth. In ancient times, the people intercoursed themselves. Later, they split to develop human man and woman.

However, the stars, the world of stars, are the background of the human world. We are all strangers here; we have come from something and somewhere else. Some people have lost their connection to their origin, so they cannot go back now. We value the ancient record, not from the standpoint of religious promotion, but because we can always discover something else about our background: a clue about general spiritual reality in the small scope of human life.

Q: You mean originally there was only one form of human being, and later they split to be two kinds, man and woman? It makes a lot of sense, because men's and women's bodies are very similar.

Master Ni: I would like to show you some simple drawings that can carry you a little deeper than language can. These charts describe this kind of development of the universe.

The infinite, the formless, the indistinguishable oneness, the parentless, Hun Tun, the foggy energy mass, the Tao. The undivided Potency, all containing all. The source, the subtle origin:

(Figure 1)

The Union of Yin and Yang

(Figure 2)

Note: Principally, Yang energy means what is apparent, what in the light, positive, masculine, etc. Yin energy means hidden, that which comes along as a side reaction to the movement of Yang energy. It exhibits supportiveness, assistance, continuation, help, accomplishing ability, receptiveness, stillness and femininity. Sometimes yin just means a different or opposite type of energy to the main energy. The two categories may demonstrate either harmony or contention. Harmony means the normalcy of nature. Contention means to bring forth destruction for renewal. Tao is expressed or exhibited in the shift from abnormal to normal in nature.

In reading the diagrams below, the two sides of the yin/yang diagrams may be reversed, as follows:

(Figure 3)

Either way is correct. Figure 2 shows the customary, standard way of reading a diagram.

Generally, there are two types of mind. Typically, the Eastern mind customarily reads the diagram as positioned in Figure 2. The other type of mind, the Western mind, habitually reads the diagram as positioned in Figure 3. Here is another example of the two tendencies of mind that show how the two minds see or read things differently. In the Chinese region, the direction South is placed at the top of a sky map, with the other directions corresponding (Figure 4). In the English speaking world, the direction North is placed at the top of a sky map, with the other directions corresponding (Figure 5).

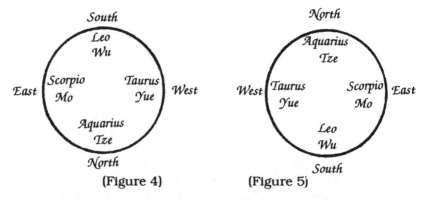

(Figure 4)   (Figure 5)

Both are correct, but merely show a different habitual tendency of mind.

The following yin/yang diagrams have been drawn for reading by the Eastern brain as that is where they originated. It may be beneficial for Western readers to turn the diagrams upside down for easier understanding if they need to do so.

The Cosmic Egg

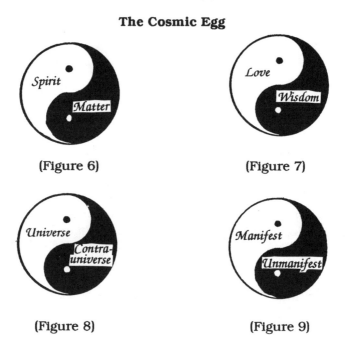

(Figure 6)   (Figure 7)

(Figure 8)   (Figure 9)

(Figure 10)

(Figure 11)

The Father and Mother in One

(Figure 12)

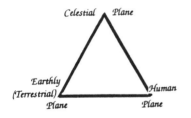

(Figure 13)

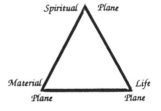

(Figure 14)

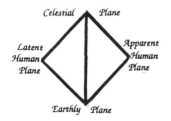

(Figure 15)

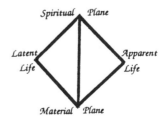

(Figure 16)

The Four Forces

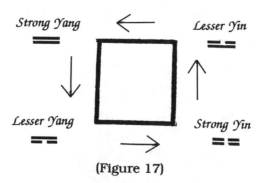

(Figure 17)

The Four Elements

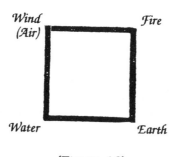

(Figure 18)

The Macrocosm with Yang and Yin Energy

(Figure 19)

The Microcosms of Yin and Yang

(Figure 20)

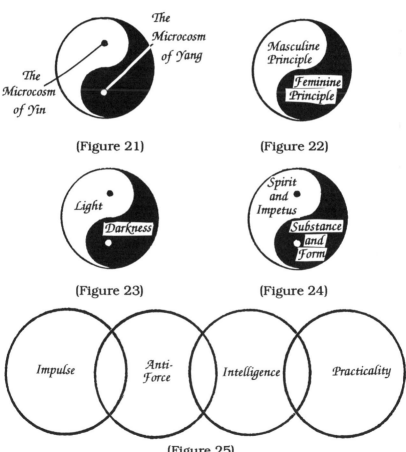

(Figure 21)

(Figure 22)

(Figure 23)

(Figure 24)

(Figure 25)

Achievement

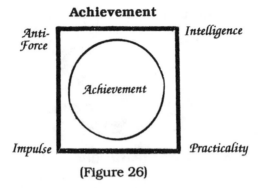

(Figure 26)

Unity and Convergence

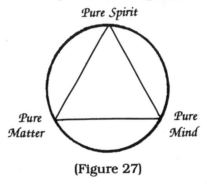

(Figure 27)

Five Elements

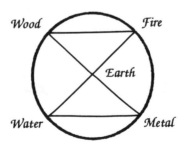

(Figure 28)

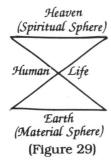

Heaven
(Spiritual Sphere)

Human — Life

Earth
(Material Sphere)

(Figure 29)

A person gives one's understanding to my work usually based on the level of vibration he is reaching through his life and cultivation. If there is an intuitive feeling that this description may be true, then your vibration may have reached a higher frequency. Some people of less strong vibration think that this is difficult to comprehend. I might like to advise to them to continue their cultivation. The ancient mythology in original Taoism was taught to the sharp minds. A wise one knows this means using the white to help the yolk by working together to obtain the higher integration. The yolk means the soul. The white means the flesh. Thus, further, higher evolution is able to reach the Inner Light and to be the Inner Light.

If you are not achieved, it is you who are still making trouble for yourself. You may wonder why I work without asking special material reward. I am happy to see the real progress of human society.

In ancient spiritual custom, it was needful for a spiritual student to donate the valuables he had, such as personal wealth, personal service and personal life to the teacher, just to learn a small insignificant practice. In modern times, some spiritual teachers also might require the same. The publication of my work, however, is not commercially oriented. It is meant to serve those who are unable to come to the meetings and gatherings. I look at my wish that the world shall have the same improvement in spiritual development as it does in material development; it is because you are one very important member of the world. I believe the teaching of my tradition possesses everlasting value, and is needed, so I offer it to you as a gift, rather than a sale.

As I see it, in ancient times, there were only a few achieved persons. This fact did not greatly help the entire society. The goal of my writing is the growth of the entire society, so that many can achieve the same spiritual level rather than just a few. This will bring true improvement to human society. Therefore, I welcome anyone to learn from my teaching. The real benefit in receiving it, however, still belongs to those who have the most sincerity and persistence.

BOOKS IN ENGLISH BY MASTER NI

Guide to Inner Light - New Publication!
Modern life is controlled by city environments, cultural customs, religious teachings and politics that can all divert our attention away from our natural life being. As a result, we lose our perspective of viewing ourselves as natural completeness. This book reveals the development of ancient Taoist adepts. Drawing inspiration from their experience, modern people who are looking for the true source and true meaning of life can find great teachings to direct and benefit them. The invaluable ancient Taoist development can teach us to reach the attainable spiritual truth and point the way to the Inner Light. Master Ni uses the ancient high accomplishments to provide this book as a useful source of our life spirit, which we have lost. 192 pages. 173 pages. Stock No. bgui. Softcover, $12.95

Stepping Stones for Spiritual Success
In Asia, the custom of foot binding was followed for close to a thousand years. In the West, people did not practice foot binding, but they bound their thoughts, for a much longer period, some 1,500 to 1,700 years. Their mind and thinking became unnatural. Being unnatural expresses a state of confusion where people do not know what is right. Once they become natural again, they become clear and progress is great. Master Ni invites his readers to unbind their minds; in this volume, he has taken the best of the traditional teachings and put them in to contemporary language to make them more relevant to our time, culture and lives. 160 pages. Stock No. BSTE. Softcover, $12.95.

The Complete Works of Lao Tzu
Lao Tzu's Tao Teh Ching is one of the most widely translated and cherished works of literature in the world. It presents the core of Taoist philosophy. Lao Tzu's timeless wisdom provides a bridge to the subtle spiritual truth and practical guidelines for harmonious and peaceful living. Master Ni has included what is believed to be the only English translation of the Hua Hu Ching, a later work of Lao Tzu which has been lost to the general public for a thousand years. 212 pages. Stock No. BCOM. Softcover, $9.95

Order The Complete Works of Lao Tzu and the companion Tao Teh Ching Cassette Tapes for only $20.00. Stock No. ABLAO.

The Book of Changes and the Unchanging Truth
The first edition of this book was widely appreciated by its readers, who drew great spiritual benefit from it. They found the principles of the I Ching to be clearly explained and useful to their lives, especially the helpful commentaries. The legendary classic I Ching is recognized as mankind's first written book of wisdom. Leaders and sages throughout history have consulted it as a trusted advisor which reveals the appropriate action to be taken in any of life's circumstances. This volume also includes over 200 pages of background material on Taoist principles of natural energy cycles, instruction and commentaries. New, revised second edition, 669 pages. Stock No. BBOO. Hardcover, $35.95

The Story of Two Kingdoms
This volume is the metaphoric tale of the conflict between the Kingdoms of Light and Darkness. Through this unique story, Master Ni transmits the esoteric teachings of Taoism which have been carefully guarded secrets for over 5,000 years. This book is for those who are serious in their search and have devoted their lives to achieving high spiritual goals. 122 pages. Stock No. BSTO. Hardcover, $14.95

The Way of Integral Life
This book can help build a bridge for those wishing to connect spiritual and intellectual development. It is most helpful for modern educated people. It includes practical and applicable suggestions for daily life, philosophical thought, esoteric insight and guidelines for those aspiring to give help and service to the world. This book helps you learn the wisdom of the ancient sages' achievement to assist the growth of your own wisdom and integrate it as your own new light and principles for balanced, reasonable living in worldly life. 320 pages. Softcover, $14.95, Stock No. BWAYS. Hardcover, $20.95, Stock No. BWAYH

Enlightenment: Mother of Spiritual Independence
The inspiring story and teachings of Master Hui Neng, the father of Zen Buddhism and Sixth Patriarch of the Buddhist tradition, highlight this volume. Hui Neng was a person of ordinary birth, intellectually unsophisticated, who achieved himself to become a spiritual leader. Master Ni includes enlivening commentaries and explanations of the principles outlined by this spiritual revolutionary. Having received the same training as all Zen Masters as one aspect of his training and achievement, Master Ni offers this teaching so that his readers may be guided in their process of spiritual development. 264 pages. Softcover, $12.95, Stock No. BENLS. Hardcover, $18.95, Stock No. BENLH

Attaining Unlimited Life
The thought-provoking teachings of Chuang Tzu are presented in this volume. He was perhaps the greatest philosopher and master of Taoism and he laid the foundation for the Taoist school of thought. Without his work, people of later generations would hardly recognize the value of Lao Tzu's teaching in practical, everyday life. He touches the organic nature of human life more deeply and directly than that of other great teachers. This volume also includes questions by students and answers by Master Ni. 467 pages. Softcover, $18.95, Stock No. BATTS; Hardcover, $25.95, Stock No. BATTH

The Gentle Path of Spiritual Progress
This book offers a glimpse into the dialogues of a Taoist master and his students. In a relaxed, open manner, Master Ni, Hua-Ching explains to his students the fundamental practices that are the keys to experiencing enlightenment in everyday life. Many of the traditional secrets of Taoist training are revealed. His students also ask a surprising range of questions, and Master Ni's answers touch on contemporary psychology, finances, sexual advice, how to use the I Ching as well as the telling of some fascinating Taoist legends. Softcover, $12.95, Stock No. BGEN

Spiritual Messages from a Buffalo Rider, A Man of Tao
This is another important collection of Master Ni's service in his worldly trip, originally published as one half of The Gentle Path. He had the opportunity to meet people and answer their questions to help them gain the spiritual awareness that we live at the command of our animal nature. Our buffalo nature rides on us, whereas an achieved person rides the buffalo. In this book, Master Ni gives much helpful knowledge to those who are interested in improving their lives and deepening their cultivation so they too can develop beyond their mundane beings. Softcover, $12.95, Stock No. BSPI

8,000 Years of Wisdom, Volume I and II
This two volume set contains a wealth of practical, down-to-earth advice given by Master Ni to his students over a five year period, 1979 to 1983. Drawing on his training in Traditional Chinese Medicine, Herbology, Acupuncture and other Taoist arts, Master Ni gives candid answers to students' questions on many topics ranging from dietary guidance to sex and pregnancy, meditation techniques and natural cures for common illnesses. Volume I includes dietary guidance; 236 pages; Stock No. BEIG1 Volume II includes sex and pregnancy guidance; 241 pages; Stock No. BEIG2. Softcover, Each Volume $12.95

The Uncharted Voyage Towards the Subtle Light

Spiritual life in the world today has become a confusing mixture of dying traditions and radical novelties. People who earnestly and sincerely seek something more than just a way to fit into the complexities of a modern structure that does not support true self-development often find themselves spiritually struggling. This book provides a profound understanding and insight into the underlying heart of all paths of spiritual growth, the subtle origin and the eternal truth of one universal life. 424 pages. Stock No. BUNC. Softcover, $14.95

The Heavenly Way

A translation of the classic Tai Shan Kan Yin Pien (Straighten Your Way) and Yin Chia Wen (The Silent Way of Blessing). The treaties in this booklet are the main guidance for a mature and healthy life. The purpose of this booklet is to promote the recognition of truth, because only truth can teach the perpetual Heavenly Way by which one reconnects oneself with the divine nature. 41 pages. Stock No. BHEA. Softcover, $2.95

Footsteps of the Mystical Child

This book poses and answers such questions as: What is a soul? What is wisdom? What is spiritual evolution? The answers to these and many other questions enable readers to open themselves to new realms of understanding and personal growth. There are also many true examples about people's internal and external struggles on the path of self-development and spiritual evolution. 166 pages. Stock No. BFOO. Softcover, $9.95

Workbook for Spiritual Development

This book offers a practical, down-to-earth, hands-on approach for those who are devoted to the path of spiritual achievement. The reader will find diagrams showing fundamental hand positions to increase and channel one's spiritual energy, postures for sitting, standing and sleeping cultivation as well as postures for many Taoist invocations. The material in this workbook is drawn from the traditional teachings of Taoism and summarizes thousands of years of little known practices for spiritual development. An entire section is devoted to ancient invocations, another on natural celibacy and another on postures. In addition, Master Ni explains the basic attitudes and understandings that are the foundation for Taoist practices. 224 pages. Stock No. BWOR. Softcover, $12.95

Poster of Master Lu

Color poster of Master Lu, Tung Ping (shown on cover of workbook), for use with the workbook or in one's shrine. 16" x 22"; Stock No. POS. $10.95

The Taoist Inner View of the Universe
This presentation of Taoist metaphysics provides guidance for one's own personal life transformation. Master Ni has given all the opportunity to know the vast achievement of the ancient unspoiled mind and its transpiercing vision. This book offers a glimpse of the inner world and immortal realm known to achieved Taoists and makes it understandable for students aspiring to a more complete life. 218 pages. Stock No. BTAOI. Softcover, $12.95

Tao, the Subtle Universal Law
Most people are unaware that their thoughts and behavior evoke responses from the invisible net of universal energy. The real meaning of Taoist self-discipline is to harmonize with universal law. To lead a good stable life is to be aware of the actual conjoining of the universal subtle law with every moment of our lives. This book presents the wisdom and practical methods that the ancient Chinese have successfully used for centuries to accomplish this. 165 pages. Stock No. TAOS. Softcover, $7.95

MATERIALS ON TAOIST HEALTH, ARTS AND SCIENCES

BOOKS

The Tao of Nutrition by Maoshing Ni, Ph.D., with Cathy McNease, B.S., M.H. - Working from ancient Chinese medical classics and contemporary research, Dr. Maoshing Ni and Cathy McNease have compiled an indispensable guide to natural healing. This exceptional book shows the reader how to take control of one's health through one's eating habits. This volume contains 3 major sections: the first section deals with theories of Chinese nutrition and philosophy; the second describes over 100 common foods in detail, listing their energetic properties, therapeutic actions and individual remedies. The third section lists nutritional remedies for many common ailments. This book presents both a healing system and a disease prevention system which is flexible in adapting to every individual's needs. 214 pages. Stock No. BTAON. Softcover, $14.95

Chinese Vegetarian Delights by Lily Chuang
An extraordinary collection of recipes based on principles of traditional Chinese nutrition. Many recipes are therapeutically prepared with herbs. Diet has long been recognized as a key factor in health and longevity. For those who require restricted diets and those who choose an optimal diet, this cookbook is a rare treasure. Meat, sugar, diary products and fried foods are excluded. Produce, grains, tofu, eggs and seaweeds are imaginatively prepared. 104 pages. Stock No. BCHIV. Softcover, $7.95

Chinese Herbology Made Easy - by Maoshing Ni, Ph.D.
This text provides an overview of Oriental medical theory, in-depth descriptions of each herb category, with over 300 black and white photographs, extensive tables of individual herbs for easy reference, and an index of pharmaceutical and Pin-Yin names. The distillation of overwhelming material into essential elements enables one to focus efficiently and develop a clear understanding of Chinese herbology. This book is especially helpful for those studying for their California Acupuncture License. 202 pages. Stock No. BCHIH. Softcover, 14.50

Crane Style Chi Gong Book - By Daoshing Ni, Ph.D.
Chi Gong is a set of meditative exercises that was developed several thousand years ago by Taoists in China. It is now practiced for healing purposes, combining breathing techniques, body movements and mental imagery to guide the smooth flow of energy throughout the body. This book gives a more detailed account and study of Chi Gong than the videotape alone. It may be used with or without the videotape. Includes complete instructions and information on using Chi Gong exercise as a medical therapy. 55 pages. Stock No. BCRA. Spiral bound $10.95

VIDEO TAPES

Crane Style Chi Gong (VHS) by Dr. Daoshing Ni, Ph.D.
Chi Gong is a set of meditative exercises developed several thousand years ago by ancient Taoists in China. It is now practiced for healing stubborn chronic diseases, strengthening the body to prevent disease and as a tool for further spiritual enlightenment. It combines breathing techniques, simple body movements, and mental imagery to guide the smooth flow of energy throughout the body. Chi gong is easy to learn for all ages. Correct and persistent practice will increase one's energy, relieve stress or tension, improve concentration and clarity, release emotional stress and restore general well-being. 2 hours Stock No. VCRA. $65.95

Eight Treasures (VHS) - By Maoshing Ni, Ph.D.
These exercises help open blocks in a person's energy flow and strengthen one's vitality. It is a complete exercise combining physical stretching and toning and energy conducting movements coordinated with breathing. The Eight Treasures are an exercise unique to the Ni family. Patterned from nature, the 32 movements of the Eight Treasures are an excellent foundation for Tai Chi Chuan or martial arts. 1 hour and 45 minutes. Stock No. VEIG. $49.95

Tai Chi Chuan - I & II (VHS) By Maoshing Ni, Ph.D.
This exercise integrates the flow of physical movement with that of integral energy in the Taoist style of "Harmony," similar to the long form of Yang-style Tai Chi Chuan. Tai Chi has been practiced for thousands of years to help both physical longevity and spiritual cultivation. 1 hour each. Each Video Tape $49.95. Order both for $90.00. Stock Nos: Part I, VTAI1; Part II, VTAI2; Set of two, VTAISET.

AUDIO CASSETTES

Invocations: Health and Longevity and Healing a Broken Heart By Maoshing Ni, Ph.D. This audio cassette guides the listener through a series of ancient invocations to channel and conduct one's own healing energy and vital force. "Thinking is louder than thunder." The mystical power by which all miracles are brought about is your sincere practice of this principle. 30 minutes. Stock No. AINV. $5.95

Chi Gong for Stress Release By Maoshing Ni, Ph.D.
This audio cassette guides you through simple, ancient breathing exercises that enable you to release day-to-day stress and tension that are such a common cause of illness today. 30 minutes. Stock No. ACHIS. $8.95

Chi Gong for Pain Management   By Maoshing Ni, Ph.D.
Using easy visualization and deep-breathing techniques that have been developed over thousands of years, this audio cassette offers methods for overcoming pain by invigorating your energy flow and unblocking obstructions that cause pain.   30 minutes.   Stock No. ACHIP. $8.95

Tao Teh Ching Cassette Tapes
This classic work of Lao Tzu has been recorded in this two-cassette set that is a companion to the book translated by Master Ni. Professionally recorded and read by Robert Rudelson. 120 minutes. Stock No. ATAO. $15.95

Order Master Ni's book, The Complete Works of Lao Tzu, and Tao Teh Ching Cassette Tapes for only $20.00. Stock No. ABLAO.

INDEX